About the author

Norman Viles was brought up in Filey on the Yorkshire coast. He has worked as a quantity surveyor and as a cost engineer on major construction projects throughout the north of England and abroad. His sea fishing stories have been published in angling and countryside interest magazines, and he also writes poetry. Norman is married to Julie, a qualified radiographer/ultrasonographer and a successful exhibitor and judge in the dog show world. They live in Filey.

Filey Brigg, showing the Brigg itself, Carr Naze (the headland), Filey Bay with resort of Filey beyond

DARK NIGHTS: WHITEWATER

Norman A. Viles

Book Guild Publishing
Sussex, England

First published in Great Britain in 2015 by
The Book Guild Ltd
The Werks
45 Church Road
Hove, BN3 2BE

Typesetting in Garamond by
Nat-Type, Cheshire

Printed in Great Britain by
CPI Antony Rowe

A catalogue record for this book is available from
The British Library.

ISBN 978 1 910508 29 9

Contents

Preface   vii

Prologue: Filey, January 1973   1

Early Years, 1950–1957   9

The Christmas Trot   17

Fishing in Filey   23

Ireland, 1962–1976   33

Conger Rock   43

Return to Ireland   51

A Taste of Irish Cream   71

Amalgam   85

Thereafter, 1963–1976   101

Good Day   103

Mary Joy: A Day in the Life of a Scarborough Keelboat   109

The Casting Competition   119

Dungeness and Skipsea   137

Fish of a Lifetime   153

Good Night, Bad Night   155

The Gulley, and Winter 1971/72   167

Of Dominoes And Codling   173

Binks and Castey   183

Freak Waves   191

Winter Fishing 1974/75   203

A Disappointing End   211

Acknowledgements   215

Preface

This book is dedicated to all those with whom I have shared my sea fishing life, and without whom it would not have been as enjoyable or entertaining as it was.

This is a book of memories of a sea fishing life. It is not a book of instruction as to how to go sea fishing; there are a good many other books to help you do that. This book recalls the things that actually happened when I went sea fishing; some were amazing, some life-threatening, some unbelievable, but all I hope are readable and entertaining.

I hope that after reading this book, if you have not tried sea fishing you will want to try your hand at it, or if you are already a sea angler that it might give you an insight into things you had not thought about before, or it may evoke memories of your own that you may have forgotten.

Either way, I hope that the book is enjoyed by all who read it.

Norman A. Viles,

Filey, Summer 2014

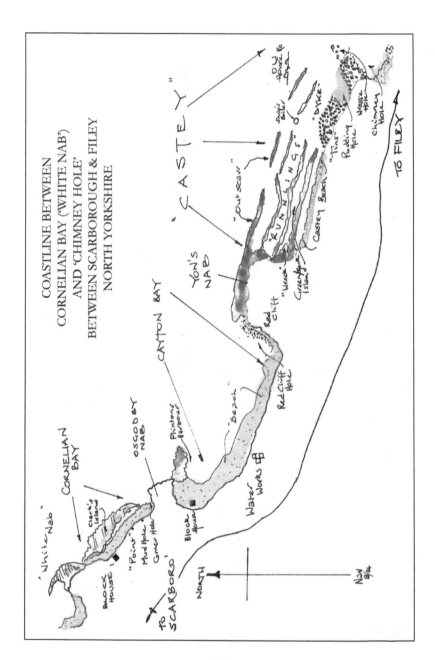

COASTLINE BETWEEN
CORNELIAN BAY (WHITE NAB)
AND 'CHIMNEY HOLE'
BETWEEN SCARBOROUGH & FILEY
NORTH YORKSHIRE

viii

FILEY BRIGG
Guide for Visitors and Anglers

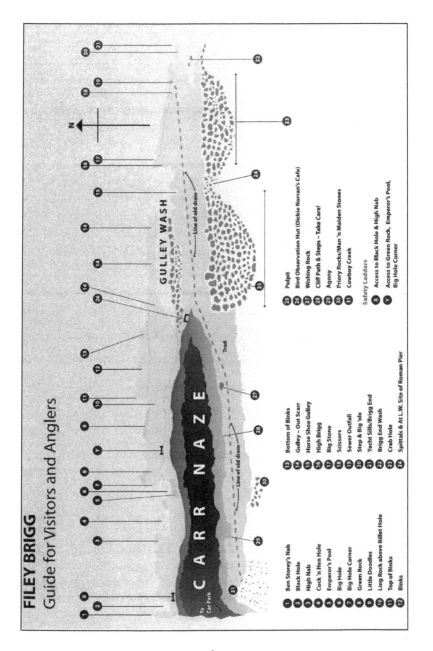

1. Ben Storey's Nab
2. Black Hole
3. High Nab
4. Cock 'n Hen Hole
5. Emperor's Pool
6. Big Hole
7. Big Hole Corner
8. Green Rock
9. Little Doodles
10. Ling Rock above Billet Hole
11. Top of Binks
12. Binks
13. Bottom of Binks
14. Gulley – Out Scarr
15. Horse Shoe Gulley
16. High Brigg
17. Big Stone
18. Scissors
19. Sewer Outfall
20. Step & Big 'ole
21. Yacht Sills/Brigg End
22. Brigg End Wash
23. Crab Hole
24. Spittals & At L.W. Site of Roman Pier
25. Pulpit
26. Bird Observation Hut (Dickie Norran's Cafe)
27. Wishing Rock
28. Cliff Path & Steps – Take Care!
29. Agony
30. Priory Rocks/Man 'n Maiden Stones
31. Cowboy Creek

Safety Ladders
X. Access to Black Hole & High Nab
Y. Access to Green Rock, Emperor's Pool, Big Hole Corner

Prologue: Filey, January 1973

It was late afternoon and the light was fading fast as I swung the car into the Carr Naze car park. Carr Naze, the landward end of Filey Brigg, is to the north of Filey, a small seaside resort halfway between Scarborough and Bridlington on the Yorkshire coast. There was as yet no moon, and away in the eastern sky stars were already showing.

I had to admit that I was a bit beat. We had started the day digging bait and then had driven south along the Holderness coast fully expecting to be able to fish one of our favourite beaches as we had the day before. But to our disappointment the bigger tide and prevailing north-east wind had produced such an onshore lift that, try as we might, we could not hold bottom and cast lines had been swept away within minutes of being put out. So, we agreed to return home, eat and then go onto Filey Brigg to fish High Nab at high water. Despite the earlier setback we were very confident of High Nab: the conditions looked just right. Biggish tide, still a bit of movement after the week's earlier blow ... yes, it should be good.

The gear unpacked, we made our way from the car park, and crossed the top of Carr Naze towards the cliff's edge. Here we stopped to turn on our headlamps and stepped down the narrow gap that leads from the cliff top to the steep path of grassy outcrops and boulder clay that would eventually bring us to the safety ladder that gave access to the sandstone scars of the cliff foot.

The climb down completed, with Fred behind me we made our way along the narrow rock path tight under the cliff face, as the sea lurched and lifted just below us. After a few moments, we were on High Nab itself.

1

'Noo den!'

The bright headlight shone directly into my eyes.

'Why, its Henry,' said Fred. 'Has't thoo dun owt, then?'

'Nahh, norra touch.' The headlight moved from my face onto Fred's. 'Anyway, thou lads, thou's in wrong spot.'

'Why?' asked Fred.

'Thou should be at Big Stone ... well, 'igh Brigg noo it's coming onto 'igh tide.'

'It's half an hour to high water, Fred,' I said.

'Aye, I know that, but we gotta ti get to High Brigg.'

'Aye,' said Henry, 'tha sooner tha betta an' all. Wish ahh could go wi' yi but ahh's due at work ternight.'

'So what's special about Big Stone, High Brigg?' I asked.

'Last night I 'ad two fish, one of nine pounds, one of just over twelve pounds, and one ah could not lift oot t' water.'

'That's it, we're off.' And Fred's light swung from Henry to me to the cliff face behind us and he'd gone back the way we had only just come.

'Thank you, Henry,' I said lifting my gear back up to my shoulders. 'We'll be seeing you. Take care.'

'Aye, and thee be canny too, there's a bit of lift tha knors.'

Even as he said it the rock beneath our feet shuddered as a heavy wave hit High Nab and roared back into the black of the night.

'Aye, you're right. Do yer reckon we'll be able to get onto High Brigg?' I asked as I turned to follow Fred, who by now was getting ready to climb the cliff ladder away to our right.

'Aye, if tha takes care!' he laughed, as he turned off his headlight.

With that I set off after Fred, knowing full well that he would not stop to get his breath back until he arrived at the end of the Carr Naze path, to face the steep path down to the Brigg itself.

It was now fully dark, and despite our headlamps we needed our full attention on the task in hand. It is a long walk from High Nab to Big Stone. First, the the climb up the safety ladder never easy when you're laden with rods, buckets and a heavy haversack. Then the steep cliff path to get back up onto Carr Naze top, some 90 feet above the sea.

2

Carr Naze, the landward end of the famous Filey Brigg is some five hundred yards in length before you reach the steep pathway down onto the Brigg itself.

I looked ahead of me, and thought about what was to come with some trepidation; I certainly was feeling weary. First, the getting down the sloping end of Carr Naze and onto the Brigg, seemingly easy, but not in the dark. But that was only half of it; what followed was a difficult trek of almost 300 yards across hard, boulder-ridden and heavy rocky ground, hoping all the time there would be no big seas coming from out of the black of a winter's night to sweep us to perdition into the bay to our right.

Fred had indeed stopped to get his breath back and was standing some way down the path that led onto the Brigg, looking out into dark, hoping to see if the pathway to High Brigg had flooded over.

'Can we get?' I asked.

I did not hear Fred's reply for as soon as I reached him he set off again. I paused and looked, but the glow of the lights from the town well away to our right gave no help as to whether or not we could get onto High Brigg safely.

I reached the bottom of the Carr Naze path with Fred 30 yards ahead of me, already off onto the Brigg itself. The further we went, the more exposed became the pathway, but although the roar of the surf was ringing in our ears a look to our left gave no inkling at all of waves crashing onto the rock scars that separated us from the sea itself.

'We're going to be lucky,' I thought, as every second brought us ever closer to High Brigg, which had now begun to materialise out of the dark ahead of us.

By now Fred had reached the turn in the pathway that gave access to High Brigg and I, heaving a huge sigh of relief at our apparent success, decided at that moment to look to my left. The headlamp swung out into the dark and for a moment that's all there was to see, a black night with an odd star. But then the shaft of light showed what I was dreading. Coming fast towards me was the wall of a wave that towered up into the night sky. Stung into action I ran as fast as my studded waders let me, and leapt the last few feet onto the rising pathway of High Brigg.

As I scrambled up the incline of the pock-marked path I looked again to my left to where I had just been. The curling top of a wave, white foam-dressed, roared past, its crest the same height as I was, and then it hit the sheer face of the path edge and fell with utter violence onto the pathway, before roaring its way into the Bay beyond.

Within seconds there was another wave, this time even bigger than the previous one, but by now I was well up the incline and had almost reached the top point of High Brigg where Fred was standing, watching both my arrival and the waves. I turned and looked back at the way we had come, and then across the bay to the lights of the town. Most of the pathway we had just crossed was awash, the waves still running on and crashing across the rocks that flank the south side of the Brigg.

'Ye gods, Fred! Did ya see that?'

'Aye, we were lucky. Just timed it right we did. Been bad to 'ave got copped by that lot.'

'Lucky? Strewth we'd 'ave been in t' bay, that's where we'd 'ave been! We'd have 'ad no chance, none. Them waves were huge, bloody ginormous!'

'Aye,' was Fred's solitary reply.

I paused to look about us and said aloud what I was thinking. 'We should be alright on 'ere though, d'yer think?'

'Aye. Should be. Its high water now, so tide'll be easing. Nay, we should be safe.'

'There were seven waves in that there run o' water. Seven, and all big uns! You know, with luck like that we might be on a winner tonight.'

'Ahh didn't count the bloody waves. And aye, tha might 'ave a point about ternight. We'll see soon enough . Now come on, let's get at it.'

I looked straight out beyond the front of High Brigg into the dark of the night and the open sea. High Brigg is the local name for the highest part of the Brigg. If you stand on the foreshore at Filey and look across the bay towards the Brigg itself, High Brigg stands up a bit like a broken tooth's edge against the long flat run of the rocky promontory that is called the Brigg. The Brigg itself is separated from the open sea beyond by a gully that holds water even at low tide. This gully is flanked on its seaward side by a long rock scarr, called localy Out Scarr, and this scarr stops with an almost vertical drop off, as if a large piece of the scarr had been cut from it, producing a wide gap in the scarr and this gap is in fact a deep hole directly in front of High Brigg.

Directly under High Brigg the scarr starts its run again and continues its way down to Brigg End, well away to our right hand. The hole is deep, filled with water at all states of the tide, fringed with extensive kelp beds and paved with rock and small stones. With direct access to the sea itself, it promises much to anglers prepared to lose some tackle in search of the big fish it certainly will attract. It is a rough hole but it was made to be fished.

I stood, and tried to both catch my breath and gather my wits as I looked about me. Before me across the bay, Filey and all its lights cast a glow that we could all but fish by, it was so bright. Fred was well on in his preparations and so I set to with a sudden enthusiasm brought on by the adrenalin rush of arriving safely, my weariness forgotten. My rod, an Abu 464, re-ringed now after years of use, was quickly assembled, the multiplier loaded with 26 lb test main line, a buckle swivel, 22 lb test hook trace, with 6/0 hook, bait a big black lugworm.

As I stood, my preparations finished, Fred was already preparing to cast; quickly looking about him he hit the swinging lead hard and away it went, disppearing into the black of the night, a deal to the right of where I had expected him to go. Then, it was my turn. Left shoulder aiming towards the hole, swinging the lead away from me in a long arc, letting the lead come back. Then as it reached the extent of its swing, pull hard with the left hand and push even harder with your right, thumb tight against the edge of the reel spool, feel the weight putting the rod into compression ... release! It flew long and high, the spool of line dropping quickly, and then there was the feel of the lead hitting the water. Stop the spool! Take up the slack line, not too much … there, it's down, and it looks to be just where I had hoped. Only time would tell. I laid the rod down, its tip projecting out over the edge of the rock, clearly visible in the ambient light. Now we waited.

It was Fred who got the first touch. It was a vigorous bite, decisive and bold, the rod tip pulled round and held down. Fred, as quick as you would expect, picked up the rod, felt the fish bite again and hit it hard, swinging the rod back and over his shoulder. The rod curved steeply. Fred began to lift the rod and reel in some line, but the fish had gone to ground, the heavy kelp giving the fish advantage, and Fred none.

We waited. Nothing. 'Its hard in, fast as a thief!' said Fred, and eventually put his rod down, the spool out of gear. We waited again, still nothing.

Then, at the edge of my vision, I saw my rod tip nod: I had a bite. Not so decisive as Fred's had been, but a good bite nonetheless. It bit again. I picked up my rod and dropped the tip, so the rod was almost horizontal, aiming out into the darkness. I gently took in the slack line, raising the rod gently. The fish bit again, the rod tip dipped hard. I struck.

'Wow!' The tip keeled over, the rod leapt into life. Thump!

Thump! A very heavy and very lively fish somewhere out in the black night began to go mad. In all truth I do not remember all the details of the next few minutes. Heaving, reeling, heaving, reeling … The reel wobbling wildly from side to side, a bloody great weight that was boring and pulling in such a way as to make the idiot who said 'Cod do not fight!' appear as relevant as moon rock to an Aborigine.

By now Fred had all but given up his own battle with the fast fish and had come to my side, holding the Tilley lamp out over the water, reaching out as far as he could to help me see the fish. And there, below our feet, came the slowly appearing shape of a very big Cod.

'Its bloody ginormous! Worra fish!' said Fred.

Watching the fish, seeing its size, numbed me. It shook its head. This spurred me into life and I sought to regain control. It came easy at first, then came a last big burst for freedom. It bore down, straight under the overhang of High Brigg itself, and again my heart stopped. But this time the fish was very tired, and as gently and patiently as I was able, I lifted the fish to the step in the scar face at the back of High Brigg. There I waited for a suitable wave to come through that would lift the fish onto the pathway we had used to get onto High Brigg. Three waves came through and each one was just not big enough to do it, but big enough to soak me. Then on the fourth wave, as it swept by me waist-deep, it took the fish up and over the scar's edge onto the pathway beyond. As the seas fell away, I ran to the flapping fish and stopped open-mouthed as I saw its size.

'Grab it, Norman, for heaven's sakes! There's a big un a-coming!' screamed Fred behind me.

I did. It was very heavy, a beautiful long deep-flanked Cod. By its colour it was newly into the kelp, with a belly that was big and rock hard. Once back up High Brigg we weighed it; it went 14 lb exactly. My best fish from the shore to that date, from a hole as rough as a badger's bottom, in a modest sea just after the top of the tide. When afterwards I gutted the fish it was full of spider crabs, which explained its hard belly.

We did not have another bite; Fred had to break out from where his fish had gone to ground, losing all his end tackle in the process. But for me, absolute delight. This had been quite a night.

'It went 14 lbs exactly. . .'

Early Years, 1950–1957

So, just how did this interest in fishing begin? Fishing for tiddlers with my granny as a child in Woodhouse Beck in Leeds, probably. Or maybe it is a part of my genetic make-up: my maternal grandfather fished, but only a little and it seems most of that was with a poacher in the Lake District. My father had no interest whatsoever. So really, if truth be told, I do not know just what it was that sparked what was to become a lifelong passion. Even as a child, removed to Filey from wartime Leeds, with the sea viewed at a distance as we walked from the train to our new temporary home, or as I played for the first time on Filey's famous beach, the sea has always fascinated me.

I was about ten when a visit from relatives to see how my family was coping resulted in my cousin and I being bought a handline each from Baxter's Chandlery in Queen Street (total cost, 5 shillings – 25p today) with which to go and fish from the seawall. Today, handlines can be very innovative and of various designs, but then it was a simple wooden frame holding some 50 yards of cotton-based line (called 'rotten bottom' by anglers everywhere today), two hooks on short catgut traces and a 6-oz sinker. We went onto the seawall down by Filey's Cobble Landing with no bait, scrounged some 'flithers' (limpets removed from their shells and used by longliners as a bait for Haddock) and tried to catch something, closely watched by some Filey fishermen who were working on their cobbles. They found our efforts highly amusing and no doubt they were, for neither of us had a clue as to what to do, nor how to do it. But we had fun learning to cast out the lead which somehow we achieved without injuring ourselves nor anyone else, I am glad to say.

It did improve; not a lot, but a bit. I eventually caught my first fish, a small Coalfish (called 'Billet' in Yorkshire), using my grandfather's old freshwater fishing gear and 'scaened' mussels as bait. The only other memory of that day was that the rod broke as the lead being used was much too heavy for an old split-cane rod to bear. But, the hook of passion had been taken and all it needed was for the hook to be set tight, and of course that eventually came about.

There were four of us. Myself, a boyhood friend, his sister and her friend, and all on a glorious summer's day. For reasons lost in the mists of time it was decided we would go fishing, and off we went with handlines onto Filey Brigg. Bearing in mind our ages – John and I were about eleven and the two girls a little younger – and that we were wearing gym shoes and flimsy summer clothing, one would have thought we would not have been allowed to do what we actually did do. But we got there safely, to find that the back of the Brigg was deserted, the sea flat calm, and we had our choice of spots to fish. We decided that a spot I later came to know as Billet Hole was the ideal place to fish. A long, relatively narrow shelf of flat rock gave us lots of room to fish and beneath our feet was 15 feet or more of water, it being low water. Bait was mussels which we sought among the rock pools about us, not that we found many, which we then smashed up since we did not know how to 'scaen' mussels of their meat, and we used bits of silver paper salvaged from a bar of chocolate which we then wrapped around the hook shank, which worked very well indeed.

We never stopped catching fish. Small Billet and some big Billet, which had we weighed them would have gone over 4 lb or even 5 lb in weight. We even caught Wrasse, which fascinated us with their many colours fresh from the sea. We put all we caught in a big pool that was directly behind us, so that by the time we made our way home the pool had the look of a well-stocked aquarium. That day, the hook was set ever more firmly.

A change of school at age eleven increased not only my interest in fishing, but also the number of friends who shared that interest. All were Filonians, born and bred, and thus all had their own fishing tackle, either handed down by parents or grandparents. In my case I had to find the wherewithal to buy it. How simple that is to say, and just how difficult it was in reality. In the event I got a 11-foot bamboo rod with zinc-plated wire rings and brass reel fittings, plus a 5-inch Scarborough reel, through the kindness of the wife of Filey's only tackle dealer, Bob Dale. Mrs Dale, bless her, let me buy both rod and reel and to pay for them as soon as I was able; no, not even regular payments, but when I could! Even today, that level of kindness and generosity to me, a 'foreigner' (a 'Wessie', West Riding-ite, recently arrived and barely welcomed), was amazing. Yes, in time I did pay it off, and was helped by my winning a Filey Brigg Angling Society (FBAS) weekly fishing competition sweep, a monetary prize which went some way to paying off my bill. But how did I, a mere novice of 14 years, achieve such a result? It came about like this ...

Bait was dug on the Saturday morning and it had been intended that two of us, John 'Tally' Abbot (who was to feature in my fishing life to a very great extent, but more of that later) and I, would fish the FBAS Match on the Sunday afternoon on the Brigg; just where, we would decide on the day. There had been some snow that week, a northerly blow, and it was cold. On calling for Tally early on the Sunday afternoon I found that he was so full of cold that he was not going to make the trip. I was disappointed, obviously, not only because I'd lost some good company, but because a decision as to where to go would have to be made by myself, and that was something I was not yet capable of doing. It is a long walk from the centre of Filey to the top of Carr Naze, the name for the cliffed part of Filey Brigg, so I had some time to decide just where I was to fish.

High water was about five o'clock, and it was a big tide with a lot of northerly still in it, which left my choices of venue somewhat limited. I decided in the end to fish from the cliff top, a location about 40 feet above the sea and directly overlooking a fishing spot called High Nab. This spot offered a number of places to put my bait: I could cast left, or straight out, or to my right into Cock 'n' Hen Hole. Not that I could cast far, anyway, but at that height I would have a great chance of catching something, or so I thought.

There was no one on High Nab Top when I arrived and so after climbing down from the cliff top onto the Top I got myself organised and on time, 1.30 p.m., made my first cast. The sea was easing, but it was still rough. Heavy swells rolled in from the northeast with some size and regularity (a sea condition which in this part of the world is called 'jowly') to crash with both power and some viciousness against the cliff foot below me. The size and strength of the waves was such that as they made their way to my right hand and further down tide to sweep across the rock scars of Filey Brigg, they made fishing from the low scars of the back of the Brigg dangerous if not impossible. I had made the right decision as to where to go, but my problem was that if I got into a good fish, just how would I manage to deal with it on a cliff top with a raging sea below me? My concerns were quickly answered as down the cliff came someone I vaguely knew by sight, who was something of a stalwart of the local fishing scene: Henry Moulson.

After the briefest of pleasantries Henry tackled up and cast his bait of mussels into Cock 'n' Hen Hole to our right, whereas mine had been cast straight off the Nab. And so we settled down to watch and wait. To our surprise it was a long wait, and we both had several casts before the first bite came. This time I had cast a deal further and more to my left than before, whilst Henry persisted in fishing Cock 'n' Hen Hole. My rod was supported on a pair of garden canes tied together to form a rod stand, which meant that my rod tip was about 4 feet above the ground. Suddenly, the rod tip dipped and sprung back, only to dip again. I saw it, but if truth be known I was so surprised at such a bite on my rod and not on Henry's that it took a shout from Henry himself to wake me from my stupor.

I carefully picked up my rod, the cane stand falling over and almost falling down the cliff face, which made me stumble as I tried to both hold the rod properly and save my rod stand. Not a glorious start to what was to follow. I stood there, the rod tip now held out over the cliff's edge, and waited. It was not long in coming: a sharp downward pull on the rod tip. I struck, lifting the rod as high as it would go, and immediately felt a heavy weight pulling my rod tip downwards.

'You've gorrit, 'ave yer?' asked Henry, standing by my right hand.

'Yerrs, I've gorrit. It's coming!' as I started to wind the reel and lift the rod as the same time.

'Grund is clean where thee put yer bait, thou should be alreet. But be canny, lad, daren't rush it. Gerrit to cliff's foot and ay'll 'elp thee gerrit up t' cliff!' continued Henry.

At this I was greatly relieved, because I'd never had a fish this size on my rod and though I was sure the rod and the reel could cope with it, Henry's words were a great encouragement. We both looked down into the grey, heaving, foam-flecked waters to see if we could spot the fish coming in, and we did – at least Henry did. A flash of white against the grey, twisting and turning as it came up from the depths.

'Be bloody careful now, lad, ease it off till this sea has gone thro', then reel like buggery and lift it!'

I did as I was told. The initial heaviness of the fish was a deal easier now that I had got it up and in towards the cliff foot. As the fish got ever closer to the rock face my heart was pounding so much it seemed I could hardly breathe. Then I saw another wave start to lift with my fish laid upon its surface. I lifted the rod as much as I could and the fish swung in and up ever closer to the rocky face of the cliff.

'Don't let it touch t' cliff!' yelled Henry, who reached out and grabbed my line. In an instant he was on his knees and then laid face down on the cliff edge with my fishing line held in both his hands.

'Ah've gorrit, its coming. Looks well 'ooked!'

Hand over hand Henry lifted the fish up the cliff face while all the time I slowly reeled in the line he had retrieved as the fish came up from the water.

'Norra bad un, lad. Six-punder ah reckon.' And with that he lifted the Cod up onto the cliff top.

I fell on it with absolute delight. My very first Cod, a beautiful gold-speckled, light-grey-backed and white-bellied fish that was indeed well hooked.

'Is tha' in t' competishun?' asked Henry.

'Yes, I am!' I replied, suddenly aware of what that could mean.

'Its after four noo. Lad, tha wants to get thisen off 'ome and then gerrit weighed in in good time, tha knows!'

I did not need any persuading and I was off as soon as I could pack up my gear and leave.

To my great surprise and delight that Cod weighed in at 6 lb 5 oz, no monster but to me a great prize, and it brought a lot of personal satisfaction and some street cred. And it won the FBAS's weekly competition and sweep. I had expected there to have been a lot of good fish caught in such excellent fishing conditions, but there were not, and my fish was the best landed that week. My affection for Henry and what he did for me that Sunday, now so long ago, has remained with me all my life; for it is certain that no matter how well hooked that fish was, I very much doubt that I had either the physical strength or the wherewithal to get that fish up to the top of High Nab entirely on my own. And I doubt the bamboo rod would have stood it either.

That self-same month, January, saw another memorable day, but this time with Tally. The northerly sea still persisted, so much so that it seemed to us both that the back of the Brigg was not the place to be, so we went to fish Crab Hole. Crab Hole is the bay side of the end of Filey Brigg. It stretches from behind High Brigg (a place called Spittals) all the way to Brigg End. Whereas the seaward side of the Brigg is a wide sloping area of flat rock, the bay side is a jumble of large boulders that makes access to the sea's edge, walking across these boulders, difficult. We arrived just after low water and made our base about halfway between Spittals and the end of the Brigg. The sea was big: huge rollers with breaking crests were sweeping into the bay between the Brigg's end and Bell Buoy, locally called Tideway. Behind us, the seaward side of the Brigg was under continous assault, with waves lifting and breaking almost continuously against the rock scars. I remember being quite apprehensive about where we were, especially as the tide was making. When the time came to get out of our spot it was not just a matter of doing this safely, it was also a battle not to get soaked, especially as we were running the gauntlet of High Brigg at its low point where the waves would soon be sweeping past the high scar and into the bay itself.

In the event, on my first cast I took a small Codling, about 2 lb, and we both felt that we could be in for a memorable day. We were, but for all the wrong reasons. Just after I had taken the Codling it started to snow heavily, and large flakes made up a blizzard of white that quickly began to cover the rocks about us, and of course ourselves and our tackle and bags

As the day and tide progressed, the rods stood unmoving with not another bite between us, until Tally said we should go to Pulpit and try there as it just might be worth our while. We got our gear together as quickly as we could and set off, crossing the snow-covered boulders, now even more hazardous, with even greater care than usual. We soon reached the backside of High Brigg, and its temporary shelter from the heavy breaking waves that were by now crashing down onto the top of the scars to our right. In that blizzard we kept a weather eye on the threat of the heavy seas, which added even more of a danger than had it been clear weather. Eventually, the assault of heavy sea paused, the so-called seventh wave effect, giving us enough time to run the feared gauntlet and on past High Brigg back towards Carr Naze and access to Pulpit.

Fishing Pulpit is much like fishing Crab Hole. Pulpit is made up of a mass of large and small boulders that flank the bay side of the Brigg from Spittals to the start of Carr Naze; again it is an east to south-east sea venue, fishing onto the soft sand of the bay using worms or mussels as bait. In our case we were using lugworm dug the previous weekend, and they were as good a bait as you could find. Once settled, we again cast out and began to wait, and the snow continued to fall, heavier than even before if that were possible. Soon we both took on the look of mobile snowmen; and our rods remained unmoving, to our surprise.

Suddenly, Tally's rod was pulled over, clattering down onto the rocks with such force that Tally, quickly picking it up, checked the rod over for broken rings (his rod was a mere 9 feet long, a Victorian relic, that had ceramic rings held in place with heavy-gauge wire, and very susceptible to breakage), but all was well. As he brought the rod back to the upright position and began to get it erect again in the rod hole he had made, the rod was pulled over firmly.

'Ye gods!' said Tally. 'Its a bloody fish!'

The rod was as stiff as a poker but even so it took on a curve as Tally braced himself with one foot against a small boulder, the other on a limpet-encrusted flat bit of scar. With the making tide and the big sea the fish gave us both some heart-stopping moments until at last Tally had pulled it almost to our feet. A heavy, white-bellied Cod, cream and speckled with soft gold spots, it went just over 9 lb. We were euphoric.

After a little time we decided that despite the temptation to stay on, getting home was going to be a struggle unless we left there and then. And so it proved.

It was still snowing as hard as it had been three hours before, and it was now really cold. It took us over three hours to get home, a walk of usually 25 minutes at the most. The high tide had cut off our escape along the side of the Brigg and onto the beach, so we had to climb the cliff in order to get onto Carr Naze and then start our walk back to Filey. That climb took us a good hour to complete, nor was the climb made any easier as Tally had the only lamp, a headlamp. On reaching the top of Carr Naze we were utterly knackered but had yet to walk back along the cliff tops to Filey itself. Here the snow was about 4 inches deep and drifting with it. We arrived home at about eight o'clock, both of us wet through and out on our feet. Despite our 'success' we both received a serious telling off from both sets of parents.

Tally's mum baked the Cod *sans* head, tail and entrails and it was served with mashed potatoes and vegetables. I cannot remember now how my small Codling was prepared, but it was surely eaten. That day is as sharp a memory now as it was that January day in 1953.

Fishing with rod and line was one thing that fascinated me, but there were other interests too, apart from the obvious ones like the opposite sex! Probably a 'trot' provided some of that interest.

16

The Christmas Trot

It was Tally who suggested that we had the 'trot'.

'Tides are just right, Norman, absolutely perfect!' he said with a zeal that was infectious. 'We'll go gravin' in t' morning, mek t' trot in t' afternoon, and lay it timorrow neet.'

Although I was as keen as Tally, I doubted that I would be able to get the time off from my family's shop as easily as that. After all it was the Thursday before Christmas week, and now that school had broken up, it was inevitable that I would have to help with making of holly wreaths or running errands or whatever else I was called upon to do.

'I'll meet thee at Bridge 'ole in t' morning, then,' I said hopefully.

'Reet. An' daint be late, low water's at nine or thereabouts and it's a big tide an' all. Aye, absolutely perfect providing we daint have a too hard a frost so's worrums won't calve.'

In the event I was there on time and my worries about helping in the shop had vanished as my services would not be required until the start of Christmas week itself. As Tally had predicted it was indeed a big tide, and the tall steel marker post that was positioned on Filey beach was some 80 yards up from the low water mark that morning.

Despite the overnight frost the lugworms were plentiful, with large symmetrical casts ('calvings') visible almost everywhere over the hard-packed sand. In Filey lugworms are called 'gullies', and the digging of them is an art form in itself. One 'graved' for 'gullies'; that meant that the hole you had to dig to catch them was both deep and quite narrow, giving the image of a grave when it had been correctly worked and the worm caught. Not only was it back-breaking work, but you had to be very quick in working your fork through the sand, for the 'gullie' sped down through its preformed hole at a very fast rate indeed.

'Ar's yer done, then?' asked Tally as I tried to straighten a back that felt like it would never be upright ever again.

'About thirty or so, an' all good uns.'

'Aye, ah got aboot same. Look, putten yours away in paper for fishing on Sat'day, an' we'll use mine for t' trot.'

''Ow many do yer reckon we'll need for t'trot, then?' I asked.

'Oh! About twenty a tide, we cud use less on 'em if we'd a mind t' use less 'ooks, but twenty hooks's abowt reet.'

A 'trot', or a nightline as it is sometimes called, is a baited set of hooks, as few as a dozen or as many as 100, tied to a length of strong line which is then laid and secured at a low water mark that from experience will hold fish whilst the tide floods then ebbs over it. It took Tally and me about an hour to make up the trot, using a length of longline begged from a local fishing family, with 20 hooks, each hook tied to a 2-foot trace tied to the longline every 2 yards or so. Tally carefully wound the trot into a neat coil and put the lot into a brown paper carrier bag.

'Where are we going t' get bricks to secure ends of line?' I asked Tally.

'Nay, thee needn't worry aboot that, we'll nick a couple from that pile in t' Foord's yard on our way down t' beach terneet.'

And that was exactly what we did.

It was a fine but cold night, the moon in full splendour, silver-white against the blue black of a cloudless starlit sky. As we made our way, a small flash of lights was visible against the dark of the cliffs that form the landward end of Filey's famous Brigg.

'Wonder who that is?' I asked Tally.

'No idea, but ah reckon we'll know soon enuff.'

It turned out that we were not alone in our idea to lay a trot. Two local stalwarts, George Sedman and Ben Roberts, were laying a full longline of a trot 150 yards long, with 75 baited hooks, along the beach from the side of Brigg towards Arndale on the low water mark.

Tally decided that we should lay ours parallel to theirs but 30 yards further up the beach, 'Just in case tide daint ebb as far as it should in t' mornin'.'

With both lines laid and baited it was now just a matter of waiting till the flooding tide covered both trots, and in due time this too was achieved. It was going on towards 11 p.m. before I got home, and after supper with disbelieving parents I finally got to bed as tired as I had been in a long time.

The next morning I called for Tally at about a quarter to eight and together we set off for the beach, full of high hopes.

'We're late. Yer can't risk yon trot barin' itsen afore we get to it, if there's any fish they'll be nicked for sure or gulls'll peck eyes out or otherwise spoil 'em and ah'll not have that!'

'But it's not low water till five minutes to ten and that's almost two hours away.'

'Aye, but tha don't realise that we laid our trot up t' beach and not on low water mark. Nay, we're only just in time, believe me.'

We had no sooner got to the Brigg side than George and Ben came down onto the beach and walked towards us.

'Mornin',' said George.

'Morning, George, Ben. Fine morning.'

'Aye. You seen your trot yet? Any sign at all?'

'Not yet, Ben, but I can see our marker just at the back of yon breaking wave.'

There, 30 yards out, was Tally's white-painted cork bob that he had tied to the end of the trot before we had left it the night before.

'Yours is just beyond ours,' I said.

'Aye, it is,' replied George quietly.

Now it was just a matter of being patient, and waiting. The time dragged and the ebb seemed to get ever slower, the white cork bob being forever out of reach. Eventually, 30 minutes before low water, we reached it. Heart in mouth we waded out into the gently falling surf, looking for the trot line, black against the brown of the sand. With a cry of delight Tally carefully lifted the line, running his fingers along its length until he had found the end and the sunken brick.

'You 'old on to this end, Norman,' said Tally, 'and I'll walk along the line to see if there is owt.'

'No splashes or owt is there?' I asked anxiously.

Tally did not answer, but with both George and Ben in attendance slowly lifted and checked every hook on the trot.

'Ah daint believe it. Nowt, absolutely nowt, and all the baits as we left 'em.'

'Thou were too far up t' beach, Tally,' said Ben. 'Thee only needs to be a couple of yards out of fish runs and tha'll catch nowt at all, and that's what tha's done 'ere.'

Stunned into silence, Tally and I said nothing, but just began to coil up the trot to re-lay it elsewhere.

'Dain't go yet, lads, will thee. Cos ours is all but ready for hauling,' said Ben with a smile. 'And dain't be doonharted tha' knows, cos it ain't end t' world.'

We waited in silence. The tide continued to ebb till suddenly, just at the back of the lifting wave, I saw the lift and splash of a fish's tail.

'Hey!' I cried. 'Did ya see that?'

They had, and as I looked back along the tables of water towards Arndale, to my utter amazement there, swimming in circles in the now fast-ebbing tide, were the erect dorsal fins of a lot of big fish. The excitement that I felt that morning I can still feel now, all these years later.

For 20 minutes George, Ben, Tally and I chased about the shallowing water lifting up prime Codlings, good ones, with the best going to almost 7 lb. Ben, who had gone to the last hook of the trot, found a Flounder the size of a meat salver that on seeing him had broken free of the hook and sped off through the shallow water in a bid for freedom. But he was not fast enough and Ben scooped him up into his arms with a whoop and a holler. Twenty-nine Codlings were taken on that trot, plus two great Flounders.

'What'll you do with them?' I asked.

'Sell 'em,' replied George.

In the event they could not, for it was Christmas week and no fish merchants, nor fishmongers nor fish shops, would take them. Unable to even give them away, George and Ben had no alternative but to take the only offer they had. Until then I would never have believed that pigs would eat fish, but the pigs in a local piggery had a most unusual Christmas dinner that year.

Fishing in Filey

The fishing scene in Filey was a very local thing. With my being very much a 'foreigner' (the local expression 'Wessie', for someone who came originally from the West Riding of Yorkshire, did not come into local common parlance until some 20 years later), I was tolerated at best and ignored for the rest of the time. My being a 'foreigner' was to stay with me for most of my life. When I married Julie, a local girl from a fishing family of a number of generations, I was called 'Lena Pearson's daughter's husband'! This needs to be explained. Lena was my mother-in-law, Pearson being her maiden name. The locals would not recognise her married name, Harding, as her husband, Arthur, came from Hunmanby, a village 4 miles south-west of Filey, but to real Filonians, to come from Hunmanby was as alien as coming from the planet Mars!

Looking back at those days it is obvious that to have had any kind of local family as a relative was at least a key to the door. In my case there just was no family contact, no one save those of my own age with whom I went to school and went fishing. In all, the group I fished with were just six in number, and of course all six had inherited tackle of some kind or other, but more important than that they could, for the most part anyway, go fishing with a relative who knew what it was all about. The importance of that was a pearl of great price, and although I was very aware of the importance of hands-on tuition, it was not going to happen to me. If I was to gain any level of knowledge it would be from my friends, or if I could prove my enthusiasm for the sport, from my elders and betters who I would meet whilst going fishing. And so we come to the Filey Brigg Angling Society (FBAS).

The FBAS was founded in 1922 and though much has changed from my teenage years, nowadays it still flourishes, providing a Winter Fishing Competition in the form of leagues for members, and in early September of every year a Festival for both boat and shore anglers which is very well supported indeed. I joined aged 14 and it was the start of a very important and happy period in my fishing life. In those days I was very much in awe of my fellow members, especially those elder statesmen of the society whose knowledge of the local fishing was extensive. Some had even been involved, albeit in a non-fishing way, in the Tunny fishing out of Scarborough in the 1920s and 1930s.

Over the next three years I learnt a very great deal and had fishing experiences that linger still in my memory, some hilarious, some exciting. If I were to recall them all, they would take up much of this book. The Christmas outings were memorable inasmuch as it was a day of a fishing competition with attendant sweep, usually over five hours on a making tide and at places carefully selected to provide both good fishing and a pub with food for 'afters'.

The Christmas outings went to Hayburn Wyke, 7 miles north of Scarborough, or we went to Flamborough Head, which provided fishing in a number of places both north of the Head end or to the south of the Head, like South Landing. We all had to be back at the weigh-in at a specific time, usually about 4 p.m., then when those who had caught fish had weighed in, and the prizes had been awarded, all would adjourn to the bar. A night of mayhem followed: tales of derring-do, singing, and a good time was had by all.

This period, 1954 to 1957, were years of some technological advances in the sea fishing world. Local tackle was a rod of 11 feet or 11 feet 6 inches, or even 12 feet in length, built of lancewood or greenheart or a combination of both, coupled to a hardwood 7-inch Scarborough reel. This was very heavy tackle and you had to be fit and strong to wield it effectively. Long casts taken for granted today were just not possible: 70 yards with bait was some cast, usually 50 or 60 yards with bait was the norm, and nylon monofilament had yet to come onto the market. We fished with Dolphin Cuttyhunk a green, twisted cotton-based line that was treated with a proprietary substance that coated the line and helped to improve its casting qualities with a breaking strain of 40 to 60 lb. The trouble was that after a few casts this 'silkiness' was lost, and with that loss, casting became more and more difficult and distance as a result was lost.

It must be said that in those days the fishing was a great deal better than today and it was always said that 'You don't have to cast far if you are rock fishing because the fish will always be under your feet!' There is a deal of truth in this, but it is a natural reaction of most anglers to want to cast as far as they can regardless of where they are fishing. So, the old Cuttyhunk line did work, and some cracking fish, invariably Cod, were caught on it.

When monofilament became available and was bought and used by local anglers the choice of breaking strain was invariably 60 to 80 lb with all the attendant problems of drag, but at least the line was silky smooth and flew off the reel. So, despite all the advantages that monofilament nylon line provided, they were ignored to follow old and long-held views that line had to be strong if it was to cope with rock fishing. When fibreglass rods came on the market these were discounted with utter scorn by many local rods, since 'Who wants to fish with a glass rod on a rock scar?!' Change took a long time to arrive in this part of the world.

Tally and I tried to fish FBAS competitions when we could, but it was never easy. For one thing, bait was all-important and tide times did not always suit school days so lugworm had to be forgotten and other baits used. The most important of these other baits were 'scaened' mussels, mussels in the raw state, which were the mainstay of the local winter fishing industry. It was essential to get to know the local fishing families so that when necessary you could go along and ask (almost always The Lady of the House) if they had any scaened mussels for sale. Some times you were told in no uncertain terms that they did not, but such occasions were relatively rare; invariably you were shown a bucket in their yard and told to 'Help thissens, but dain't be over greedy!' This was met with a shout of delight and the derisory payment of a few shillings, usually a couple of bob or even, if we were feeling flush, half a crown. Bearing in mind the efforts involved in the harvesting, transporting and the scaening of mussels such a payment, however valuable to us, was utterly inadequate.

Years later I discovered that my mother-in-law, Lena Harding (née Pearson), a well-known Filey character and daughter of a Filey fishing family, was at one time during the 1930s employed with her sister Jane to scaen mussels for a living. Beginning at 5 a.m. and finishing at about 8 a.m. they would scaen a hundredweight bag of mussels each for the princely sum of 2 shillings and 6 pence (12.5 pence in today's money). Even today, among those fishermen who still survive are those who remember Jane as the best scaener they ever knew. Praise indeed! If you have never done it nor seen it done, go to your local supermarket's fishmonger stand and buy a mussel. Try to open it and ensure that you do not damage the flesh of the mussel, because damaged mussels are all but impossible to keep on a hook, which is the whole purpose of the exercise. Today it is an almost lost art, as difficult and demanding a task as you can imagine, and an essential part of Filey's fishing industry for a very long time indeed.

Again a January day. We were back at school, but Wednesday for our school was a half day and we were determined to fish the FBAS match if we could. Bait had to be scaened mussels; these had to be collected en route to the Brigg so it was late when we arrived on Carr Naze. One look at the sea state told us that any idea of fishing the back of the Brigg was not going to be possible, especially as the tide continued to make, with heavy seas already surging across the flat rock scars that make up the back of Filey Brigg. So we went as usual to High Nab Top and this time we would not have it to ourselves, for two rods were already there and fishing. For me it was to be a day of misery; desperate to try and make up for lost time, and very much aware of the eyes of both local anglers watching my efforts, I tried too hard and as a result had the biggest 'backlash' (the reel over-running and spilling too much line off the reel, so it jams) I think I ever had fishing with a Scarborough reel in my whole life experience of this reel.

For the rest of that afternoon I sat on a cliff face on a shelf of clay and tried (unsuccessfully, I must add) to undo the tangled mess of line I had made with my botched cast. All afternoon right into dark, Tally, Jack Haddington (an elder statesman of the local angling scene and an old-fashioned gentleman) together with Hubert Clubley had a field day, continually it seemed to me, catching Codling up to 6 lb which to my sense of self-esteem was a continual poke in the eye with a blunt stick.

That afternoon I saw the best bite I have ever seen shown on a fishing rod. Jack had a 12-foot greenheart rod, so well made it that was much coveted by the likes of me, and coupled to a 7-inch Scarborough reel it was a very impressive piece of tackle. It was also very heavy, you had to be strong to handle it well. The rod was supported on a rod rest made up of couple of softwood battens each about 5 feet long and held together with a small butterfly bolt set about 4 feet above the pointed ends. The rod and the rest had been positioned about 10 feet away from the cliff's edge, the butt of the rod on the ground, the tip about 6 feet above the ground. There was only the slightest breeze; high water was about two hours away and the first fish had yet to arrive. There was nobody standing within 10 feet of any rod and nobody was talking.

Suddenly, Jack's rod tip was pulled down quite viciously as if someone had grabbed a handful of his line and yanked the line downward with great strength. The butt and the reel lifted a good foot into the air. The rod tip then leapt back, the reel clattered back to earth, and as the rod and stand achieved the perfect balance of butt and rod tip, the rod rest actually moved forward towards the cliff edge. Then again the rod tip was pulled down and the whole series of images repeated again. It seemed that everything then happened in slow motion, as if Jack was standing in treacle. But he grabbed the rod, lifted it, fingers groping for the reel handles, all the time the rod being pulled downward and towards the cliff edge. Jack, by now in control of the situation, responded and began to lift the rod, and struck hard! The rod came up and back until having gained only a couple of yards of line, the rod, now almost vertical, stopped dead as did the recovery of line.

27

'Dammit, I'm fast!'

Jack must have stood there for a good 20 minutes. He never spoke except maybe to himself, letting enough line out to enable the fish to move from where it had run hard aground and then waiting for the fish to take up that slack line and move out from whatever it was fast in.

It never did move. Try as he might, whatever had taken that bait did not move; Jack's line and end tackle remained unmovable. During the time Jack stood and tried to resolve the situation, nobody spoke a word. When Jack eventually took the line over his shoulder and broke his end tackle free, having kept our own counsel through it all we now muttered condolences as Jack made his way back to where his tackle bags lay to make up a set of new end tackle.

On fishing days long, long afterwards I have asked local anglers what they thought it could have been. The obvious answer by many was 'A good Cod', but occasionally someone a bit longer in the tooth and very experienced in the local angling world has said 'Conger Eel!' and having lived with this idea for some time now, I tend to agree that a big Conger was the probable cause. What Jack thought it might have been I never did discover.

It was not all winter fishing. Summer was Mackerel, first and last. But – and it is a big 'but' – the sea then had a great deal more fish in it then than five years later, and a great deal more than 10, 20, 50 years later. It was a common sight to see visitors who had gone off in any of the pleasure boats that were once numerous on Filey's Cobble Landing for a morning's fishing come back ashore with caught fish bundled together with a piece of strong cord through their gills, so many and so heavy that they could hardly carry them from boat to car. The boats would go 'Dabbing' to a spot in the bay where you can if you look westward see straight up Cargate Hill (a seaside access road in the middle of the seafront), and for your other mark, look northwards towards Scarborough, seek out Scarborough Castle and get it to peep just over the end of Carr Naze (of Filey Brigg). Once anchored there it was possible to fill a fish box with beautiful plump Dabs, all well over-sized and a joy to eat with buttered brown bread and a glass of Chablis.

If you fished Tideway, the area of seaway between the end of Filey Brigg and the Bell Buoy, there were Pollack or Coalfish (called Billet in Filey), Codling of course, and more often than not a good Cod up to 10 lb could be taken, or maybe on occasion an even bigger one. On a fine sunny day with suitable tides visitors would be taken off to fish High Rock, an area of hard rocky ground outside the limits of the bay, stretching almost as far as Flamborough Head. Here fishing was as Tideway, but with the chance of a good Haddock, big Whiting, Gurnard, and of course the ubiquitous Cod, but out here the chances were that the Cod would for the most part be bigger than those taken in Tideway.

The *Gay Gordon, Janet & Carole, Endeavour*, sometimes *Gulf Stream* if she was not Salmoning, and *Freelance* and others were all busy throughout the summer days, and did just as well in the Filey Brigg Angling Society's Annual Fishing Festival. In those days the Festival boating days attracted many entries from both competent anglers and visitors alike, so much so that every cobble (sometimes a dozen or more) plus the usual pleasure boats were involved in trying to meet the demand for spaces. The 'big boats', as the cobbles were called, did not get involved in rod and line fishing, their interests being winter lining or potting, but demand was such in those days that the big boats, would take a dozen rods, whereas the popular boats would take eight or maybe ten rods a time.

The number of contestants was often well over 150 persons, and that included both women and older children. Catches were usually good with top weights of 70 lb or more, and the best fish, invariably a Cod, in the late teens in weight.

It is only as the catches declined that change came over the Festival. Today there are no pleasure boats and the boats involved in the Festival are all privately owned, with rarely more than four rods carried at any one time. The visitor wanting a day's fishing from boats, be it summer time or at the Festival, must look to Scarborough or Bridlington and if he or she wants to go off into Filey Bay, then they must have friends among the local boat owners who are willing to take them.

I had days off in a boat; there were not many. For one thing it did cost money, and my family could not always see their way to find it for me! One summer's day in early July, sometime in the mid-1950s, I was asked by a school friend of mine – Trevor Jones with whom years later I would share ownership of *Cameron Rose* – if I wanted a day's boat fishing with him and a visitor to his family's boarding house. I of course said yes.

We went off in *Freelance*, an 18-foot long, clinker-built pleasure boat with a converted Morris 8 petrol engine, but in need of some TLC. The boat was being run by Dicky Norran, a venerable fisherman of renown who in his later days helped to run the famous Brigg Cafe. We had no bait, but as Dick said, that 'were no problem', and it was not. We stopped alongside a Salmon cobble as we made our way alongside the Brigg and took from them half a dozen Launce Eels. To this day I have no idea how a Salmon netter could have caught a Launce – a big 8-inch and more long Sand Eel. Anyway, they proved to be irresistible to every fish that came anywhere near them; and we had some feathers. We seemed never to stop catching fish: Mackerel, Horse Mackerel (as rare today as rocking horse droppings), Whiting, Coalfish and Codling. It was a wonderful initiation to boat fishing for me, and it was on this trip that I saw my first multipliying reel, a Penn, used by Trevor's guest. I remember not being impressed, but then my ignorance of fishing in those days was almost total.

My experiences with the Festival were few. One is memorable: the first day of the 1954 Festival, a Monday, and I was off in the big cobble *Jean & Barbara* with Old Jim Haxby and Mark Henry Scotter as our boatmen. We went to fish off White Rocks, fishing within 200 yards of the foot of Bempton and Buckden cliffs of Flamborough Head. Like an idiot I used my bamboo rod, all 11 feet of it, and if there is one thing you cannot do, that is to use a long rod in a small, cramped fishing space. Heaven only knows how many bites I had and missed, but it was a great many. In the event the competition was won by a Mr Cross of Hull who was fishing No. 2 to my drawn No. 1, the best two positions in a boat you can draw out of a hat. When we got to weigh in, Mr Cross had 66 lb as best I can remember, whilst I weighed in about 40 lb. Mr Cross was top weight for the day and took the Cup, and I had a lesson in boat fishing that I have never forgotten. The other memory of that day was of the gannets that dived and swooped all around *Jean & Barbara* for some time, a blizzard of white, birds' cries and the splash of the diving birds, a sight never to be forgotten. Since the number of gannets in the local colony at the foot of Bempton cliffs was no more than 25 pairs, where did the rest come from?

But summer fishing was, for me, Mackerel. This is a memory of mixed blessings. If anyone goes Mackereling today, a lightweight rod, an 8 lb line and a few lures is the usual armament. When I went, as did many others of the time, it was my bamboo pole, a Scarborough reel laden with 60 lb plus nylon line and a string of nine 'jiggers' (feathers). There were many days in my youth when the Mackerel were so prolific that you caught nine Mackerel if not on every cast, then on every other one. With rock pools full of caught fish, scars scattered with the dead bodies of discarded fish, the back of the Brigg was more like an abbatoir on a bad day. Oftentimes as you stood on a scar's edge, the sea lapping your feet, there would be Herring sile (baby Herrings) being washed up over and onto your boot tops or sandals, as they tried to escape from the many predators chasing them tight into the scar edges as the tide came ever higher.

But Mackerel were not the only fruit caught. Billet, Pollack, Codling and sometimes full-grown Cod, Launce, and Horse Mackerel – a fish so rare nowadays as to lead you to believe they are now extinct. I remember on one early summer's morning finding one of the larger rock pools on the back of the Brigg full to its brim with dead Horse Mackerel. How many there were I cannot begin to count but it was a full shoal I am sure, caught on an ebbing tide and determined to get at the trapped Herring and Sand Eels, but whereas the water was deep enough to allow the bait fish to escape it was not deep enough for the Horse Mackerel, and so they perished. On one occasion a Deal Fish was caught in a local Salmon net. This long fish (the one caught that day was over 6 feet in length) with flat sides, a bright silver fish with a large squarish head, was known as the 'King

31

of the Herring' and where a Deal Fish was, there you would find the Herring.

But those days are now gone. If not forever, then only a mighty Earthly calamity will restore the fish stocks to such an extent that those days may one day be repeated. It was normal in my youth to go to the cliff tops in late June or early July and look out across the bay and see numerous patches of white stretching from behind the Brigg all the way towards Flamborough Head where gulls were feeding on the remains of Herring and Sand Eels taken by the auks which were taking the bait fish deep beneath the sea's surface. Such a sight has not been seen in Filey for at least 30 years if not more. This is a tragedy beyond my understanding; at one time between the end of the Great War and the start of World War II at least 100,000 people were involved in the Herring fishery of Britain. Today there are not enough Herring left in the North Sea to keep 1 per cent of that many people employed for a half a day, but to hear the pleas and cries of the fishing industry, the sea is full of Herring.

As for the disappearing Sand Eels, until the Sand Eel fishery was regulated (20 years too late, in my opinion) up to 2 million tons of Sand Eels were caught by industrial fishing means every year. Once the auks and gannets could feed readily in Filey Bay or its environs on Herring and Sand Eels, but nowadays they are having to travel as far as the Dogger Bank to feed. The RSPB is firmly of the opinion that the problem with loss of food for the birds is almost entirely due to climate change. I do not agree; no fishery can sustain such an attack of industrial fishing to the extent of 2 or 3 millions tons a year and continue to be there year after year to meet such demands.

By 1956 I had left school and begun to look for employment where none existed. After three months of searching I was extremely fortunate to get a job as a junior surveyor with a national firm of quantity surveyors based in Leeds. My life would never be the same again.

Ireland, 1962–1976

It really was some kind of miracle that I persuaded two of my one-time school friends to go on holiday in Ireland. I had expected all kinds of objections to my idea, not least being the funding; there had to be a way to get to Kinsale, my chosen venue, that would not break the bank for all of us, and there were other problems too, all solvable. And we did solve them.

John Addis, Tally Abbott and myself flew from Leeds Bradford Airport on a Friday evening in early September 1962. Being our first trip abroad together it was not without difficulties, such as having to give up our long-booked seats to a group who were desperate to get to the Dublin Horse Show Grand Ball, which resulted in our staying overnight in Dublin Airport. Anyway, we survived all that and duly arrived in Kinsale.

We stayed in a caravan that was parked on the quayside in Kinsale, where today stands a luxurious four-star hotel. Mrs Green was the site manager who guided, helped and generally looked after us like an old-fashioned mother hen. It was quite a week: looking back now I find it hard to believe we did as much as we did in the eight days of our holiday.

We went off in the boats. It was fashionable for visitors to Kinsale to go boat fishing whether or not they had ever wet any kind of line before, ashore or afloat. And, of course, it was fashionable to go after Blue Shark or the big Skate for which Kinsale had become internationally famous. We had no interest whatever in Blue Sharks but maybe had a yen for the Skate, for John had caught a Common Skate of 90 lb off Kinsale the previous year whilst on holiday with his father and another friend of ours called Fred Hall. What made that catch particularly interesting, if not incredible, was that John was using his Apollo steel-cored 11-foot 6-inch rod, a rod more suitable for working on a building site or dockyard as a crane. It was a beast of a weapon, heavy and utterly unyielding, a rod more designed for Popeye's friend Bluto than for any mere mortal. John, who was a strong, well-made young man, used this rod with a 7-inch Scarborough reel, 80 lb b.s. nylon monofilament line, a steel trace with a very large hook and a side of Mackerel. How the three of them coped with a fish of such a size and weight, using such tackle, aboard a locally hired 20-foot boat, defies belief – but the three of them did it. They measured it as best they could, took photographs and then released it.

One would have thought that was enough excitement for anyone for that day, but it was only a taster. Fred, using his own Scarborough rock fishing glass fibre rod and Scarborough 7-inch reel got into an even bigger Skate, a fish so powerful and heavy that he got it to within a few feet of the boat's side on several occasions only to see the Skate disappear at a rate of knots, the unstoppable revolving reel burning Fred's thumb in the process, and doing no good to his usual steady approach to fish and fishing. It got away, and of course the result of that has been a sense of needle competition between John and Fred ever since.

There were a number of boats for hire in Kinsale complete with a skipper. The big, more famous boats – *Moonlighter*, *Rapparee* – were all fully booked for the week. Undeterred, on the Monday we went off with three other anglers from the north of Ireland and had an interesting day in which I caught three Conger Eels, two in the late 20 pounds but one of over 40 lb that went well depite the unsporting and heavy tackle that I had hired to use that day. The next day we tried for a repeat but all boats, save one, were fully booked.

In the event, Mrs Green turned up trumps. We got an excellent boatman to guide us, called of course Paddy, his surname lost now in the ether of time, if we ever knew it. The boat was called *Northern Star* and belonged to the famous documentary film maker John

Grierson. With her foredeck cabined, and an open stern, stained and varnished, this 26-foot sea boat was everything anyone could desire; we could not have been better served.

Our 'mixed' fishing gave us two days of excellent fishing over the Sovereign Rocks with Pollack to 14 lb, Ling over 20 lb, Dogfish, and the biggest Bull Huss that any of us had ever seen including Paddy. The Huss, immediately it was on the surface, began to roll violently and in doing so got ever further away from the side of the boat, making gaffing impossible. As I lifted the rod to bring it closer it rolled again and dived and my hook flew from the corner of its mouth. As I stood looking at the spot where it had just disappeared into the depths, Paddy came over and put his arm over my shoulder.

''Tis the closest I'll ever be to an Irish record!' he said.

The boat fishing had been even more successful than we had dared to hope; each time we landed in the early evening a small crowd of spectators gathered to look at and take away with them part of our catch. On the morning of our third boat trip Mrs Green told us that as a result of our successful mixed fishing trips she had had requests from the parties on the other sea fishing boats to have a go over the Sovereign Rocks, as we had. I never got to know if they were as successful as we had been.

It must be recorded that our boat trips were not without incident of some kind or another. The one that stands out in my memory was the day we went Turboting off the Old Head of Kinsale. This was John's idea; he was determined to catch his first Turbot and was sure that Kinsale could provide the relevant fishing grounds. Neither Tally nor I were sympathetic to the idea, but John was our friend and so there was no argument.

As we came out of the Kinsale Estuary and turned westwards towards the Old Head of Kinsale, sitting upon the surface of the sea directly off the headland was a patch of fog, a couple of hundred yards or more long and seemingly as deep as it was long. It was a very unusual sight on a very beautiful and sunny morning to see such a fog patch sitting upon the sea. We knew we had to fish within it, and that it was going to be cold and wet; and so it was.

We anchored and the only action of the whole morning was the movement of the boat to its anchor. Little was said but a lot of cigarettes were smoked. We'd been there for about a couple of hours and were getting very restless; there had not been any kind of bite to any rod and baits were retrieved as they had been put in, untouched. I was sitting on the transom stern, my rod laid upon my left shoulder, my sight focused on the windscreen of *Northern Star*, wondering if the fog that still lay all about us had in fact thinned or moved, because I was sure I could see much further forrard than before.

As I looked through the windscreen, suddenly there appeared a huge tail, black against the grey white of the sky and framed by part of the windscreen. I yelled out but by the time my companions turned to look there was nothing to see. We were all expectant now, my companions no doubt in disbelief, but I was in no doubt as to what I'd seen.

'What d'yer think it was?' asked John.

'A whale's tail,' I replied.

I heard Tally grunt and Paddy said something I did not catch, but as we stood in silence, all listening very hard, there came the sound of breaking water and what sounded like a short burst of flatulence.

'D'yer 'ear that?' I asked.

Silence. Then the sounds of breaking water was much closer. I turned and looked to my left and into the swirling grey fog some yards off the stern of our boat.

It came all of a sudden. One moment there was nothing there, and the next came the blunt and rounded head of what to my eyes could only be a Whale – and it was coming straight at us.

'Ye gods! It'll hit us!' I yelled out and leaned forwards over the stern rail for a closer look, as did both John and Tally, now standing beside me. The head was now no more than 10 feet away from us. The Whale came on but moved slightly to its right. We were now close enough to see that its head was scarred and scratched; at water level a dark black and amber eye looked directly at us. As the whale began to pass the stern, the whole boat moved to starboard and as it moved the stern itself lifted from the water.

As all this was going on, Paddy had left the stern-well and leapt for the control panel on the bridge. It seemed instantaneous, but as the Whale swept by our stern, with John, Tally and I, mesmerised by its presence, standing as in aspic, the roar of the diesel engine filled the air. The boat lurched and immediately we were underway!

'Get yer gear up, lads!' screamed Paddy and so aroused we each grabbed for our rods and began to wind in to retrieve our tackle. As we did so there was a sudden 'swish' as the anchor cable leapt from the sea as we passed its vertical hold on the sea bed; the boat continued in its flight and the cable, relieved of its secure hold on the bottom, now streamed out sternwards 5 feet above the sea, almost taking our heads off.

'Tha sooner we's owt of 'ere tha betta, or it'll 'ave us at da bottom o' the North Atlantic!' said Paddy.

It was some time later before he put the engine to half throttle and asked what we wanted to do now. Everything we said or decided after those events is now lost and forgotten to my memory, but not our meeting with the Whale.

Our interest in Kinsale had had its birth in the fishing reports included in the *Angling Times*, a weekly angling newspaper which for the price of 6 old pennies did its level best to report the best of coarse, game and sea fishing that had happened throughout the UK during the previous week. In these reports Kinsale featured on a regular basis. As a result of this I got to hear of a local rod who I thought may be able to help three young, keen visitors to Kinsale, but seriously ignorant of its fishing, particularly the Bass fishing. This local rod was called Tom White. Tom had been evacuated to Kinsale during the Great War, having suffered a serious facial wound. He fell in love with the place – and having seen Kinsale, who can blame him? – and decided to settle there.

Fishing had always been of great interest to him and so he began to get involved with the local fishing scene, especially rod and line fishing for Bass. His experiences of Bass fishing at Kinsale particularly (the River Brandon) are too many to be listed in any part here except to say he was very successful, and as I remember now his best fish went over 13 lb.

In the world of Bass fishing, Tom had become something of a legend in his own lifetime. I can only tell of my own experiences with Tom and what happened. I wrote to him through a 'made-up' address; I cannot remember exactly how I addressed the envelope but it would have been something like 'Mr Tom White, Bass Angler, Kinsale, Eire', and it got to him, which says volumes about the Irish Mail service and obviously Tom's reputation. So, on a bright September morning the three of us called at Tom's house where he welcomed us like long-lost friends. We agreed to go fishing with him the following morning, and so we did.

A 16-foot dinghy with a Seagull outboard and four rods aboard does not make for easy fishing, especially as we had gone to spin for Bass. No sooner had he got aboard than Tom asked me to tackle up one of his two rods as he helmed the dinghy upstream. I found a somewhat battered 8-foot solid glass rod with a small centrepin reel. I must say I did as I was told with not the best of grace, as my heart was set on spinning as soon as was possible, and the setting up of someone else's tackle was the last thing I had expected to do.

There was no bait in the dinghy but I had bought a packet of Brent's Salted Lugworm at Mrs Green's tackle shop that very morning, more in hope than in expectation, because over the years when no lugworm could be dug due to neap tides or whatever, I had bought innumerable packets of this bait all to no avail. Ripping it open, I baited up using three of the salted lugworm that did not fall apart as they were wont to, and as soon as the dinghy had slowed to a crawl and Tom told us to start fishing I picked up his rod and lowered the baited hook and sinker gently over the side and let the reel go until I felt the lead hit bottom. Then I reeled in about a couple of turns of the reel, fastened the line to a reel handle and immediately set about getting my spinning gear set up. Meanwhile John, Tally and Tom were all spinning the waters about us.

We were about 600 yards upstream of the Kinsale jetties, the river was slowing as the incoming tide pressed the river's flow as high water approached. Try as we might the four rods produced nothing whatever, and high water came and went and soon we were moving downstream again towards Kinsale and the jetties. It must have taken the bait without anyone of us seeing it, no rod tip being pulled or jerked, but suddenly Tom's baited rod plunged downward, the rod butt lifting and being pulled directly towards the dinghy's bow and, if not grabbed, over the side. Just in time, I saw it. I grabbed the rod and held on; somewhere down in that now quickly moving river was a Bass fighting for its life. Of the next five minutes I remember very little, except Tally or John doing the netting of the Bass which when weighed on an elderly rusted set of spring scales went to exactly 7 lb. I was more than delighted, and I remember Tom giving me a nod of approval which meant a deal to me at the time. So, really before we knew it the morning and its fishing had gone and we were tying up and saying our goodbyes. It would be six years before I was to see Tom White again.

It was a memorable few days' holiday. There was a keelboat tied up in the harbour called *Good Hope*, 49 feet long and commonplace on the Yorkshire coast and known for its Herring fishing capabilities. It was owned by a professional photographer called Mr Barrington Martin who spent his summers more often than not based in Kinsale, and whose sole purpose, as it seemed to us, was to catch either a national Irish (or better still a European) record Pollack.

It was inevitable that we met, and sure enough he invited the three of us to join him in his quest, particularly in fishing the wreck of the RMS *Lusitania*, the famous World War I transatlantic ocean liner that was torpedoed off the Old Head of Kinsale in 1915 with heavy loss of life.

As sea fishing as a sport grew and expanded together with the sonar and navigating technology, anglers 'discovered' sea bed wrecks and the fantastic fishing that such locations offered, with Conger Eels up to and beyond 100 lb in weight, big Cod to 40 lb, Pollack, Coalfish and so on. The wreck of the *Lusitania* was in those days still hard to find as electronic navigating equipment was still very much in its infancy, but it was well worth the effort as many specimens had already been caught.

But it was not to be, for changing weather and a rapidly moving cold front meant that both the fishing and locating the *Lusitania* would prove to be very difficult, so our trip was off, which was a disappointment. In the week following our return to the UK some anglers from Dublin had a field day with Barrington and the *Good Hope*, taking Cod to 32 lb.

If there was a downside memory of this holiday it was not because of the fishing, the weather or the people of Kinsale and Ireland. Directly in front of the caravan site, located as it was on the harbourside, was what could only be described as a fish graveyard. In an area of approximately 80 yards by 40 yards, all the fish caught in the boats but not wanted by locals to eat, or for any other reason, were dumped into this area of the harbour. A good many huge Skate that once would have weighed up to 200 lb, big blue Sharks, many well over 100 lb plus in weight, as well as large Conger Eels, some Pollack and numerous other fish lay one on another and clearly visible through the murky sheen of the blue-grey water. Today, probably – hopefully – in a more enlightened society such fish would have been returned alive, but in those days it was fashionable to be photographed with your catch hung by a large derrick hook through its gills with a chalk board beside you, giving details of your catch.

This 'graveyard' had its fans; early in the morning or late in the day, shoals of Mullet would silently swim into the area in groups of four or five. The biggest fish in the shoal would butt its head into a corpse and as pieces of flesh broke away from the carcass the fish in the shoal would investigate or take a piece before moving away into darker water. There were some very big Mullet in these shoals, certainly over 10 lb, and a few more substantial than that. These monster Mullet attracted human predators; it was usual to see someone complete with a long-shafted gaff lying prone upon a pontoon, and under the guidance of someone on the harbour wall they would launch an attack on the Mullet as they passed close by the gaff's head. In all the time we stood and watched this dramatic farce not one Mullet was scratched, and certainly not caught, despite very serious and concerted efforts made by their pursuers.

Then, there was Conger Rock ...

Conger Rock

There were four of us standing on the Kinsale Quay that morning in late August. Three Yorkshiremen – John, Tally and myself – and an Irishman. As usual during that memorable holiday, the talk was of fish and fishing.

'Well, Paddy, where should we try this afternoon?' I asked. 'Is there anywhere here we could fish from the shore and have the chance of a fish, any fish?'

'Aye,' said Paddy, 'there is, and chances of good fish there are, too. Conger Rock you want. Ah, Conger Rock, the fishes that I've had there, and lost …' His eyes glazed and he stared beyond my face into the distant past to memories still aglow in his heart, never to be forgotten.

'Look,' he said, 'you see over there, on the far side of the estuary, there's a house. You see it?'

We turned and looked – his hand pointed across the windswept estuary, past the dipping masts of yachts, twisting and darting at their moorings before the fresh westerly wind, to where a broad, green field swept down to a copse of trees, and in the copse stood a house.

'Yes, I see it.'

'Well,' said Paddy, 'about 100 yards or so to the left of that house the road sweeps nearly to the river's edge and there you'll see a gap in the hedge. Go through and you'll find a flat ledge of rock. You fish there, lads, and don't cast too far, twenty yards is more than enough.'

'Twenty yards!' said John, seemingly aghast, his ability to cast prodigious distances now of no consequence.

'Aye, twenty yards. And use big baits, lads, the bloodier the better. And good luck to you.'

With that Paddy was off across the tarmac to his waiting party of anglers. John, Tally and I turned and looked across the wide sweep of the estuary to where we thought the rock stood, but the early sun's glare made the river's edge indistinct and all we could see was the golden ribbon of sun shining out on the River Bandon as it slid past the landing to the open sea.

We had arrived at Kinsale a few days before and had been out in the big boats, with fishing the likes of which we had never known before: great, deep-bodied, bronze Pollack, heavyweight Ling, Turbot, Dogs, Skate and Mackerel by the score. But now our thoughts turned to our real love, shore fishing, and what delights could be had close at hand, now that we had savoured the boats. Since we had been with Paddy in the big boats and had found him to be a keen sea angler as well as a professional boatman, he was the obvious man to ask about the shore fishing. This we had done and Conger Rock was his answer – we would try it.

With fresh bait now our first consideration we walked across the hard standing to the landing's edge. *Rapparee* and *Moonlighter*, the big boats, were laid alongside the pontoons, a hive of hectic activity with rods, strawbags and all the other paraphernalia that goes with a day's sea angling being carried from the harbour wall across wooden gangways to the waiting boats. To our left the keelboat *Good Hope* was tied up, and having just recently met her owner we felt sure that he would let us have a few Mackerel. Sure enough, after being asked he disappeared down below and in a little while returned with a dozen plump Mackerel lying in the bottom of a fish box. If we ran short, he assured us, a spinner worked on top of the flood should produce some fresh bait.

So we left the landing and made our way over the now heat-hazed tarmac, and with the previous night's copy of the local paper quickly wrapped the Mackerel to preserve at least some of their freshness, and began then to prepare for the day. We had, of course, never fished for Conger, and to be honest the sum total of our fishing abilities was the relatively narrow world of fishing for Cod amid the kelp jungles of the Yorkshire coast, with the odd helping of summer Mackerel, Coalie and the occasional Pollack. To be truthful we were young in our sport, but nonetheless this did not halt our enthusiasm. What we did know about Congers was that they were big and would fight hard. This knowledge we had just acquired due to the fact that we had had six the day before in the boats, the best weighing at least 40 lb, caught on tackle that to us at the time was far too heavy to afford maximum sport.

Lunch was hurried. It is always so when big things are afoot, and so a little after noon, laden with rods and strawbags, we made our way through the busy, quaint little town of Kinsale to the far eastern side of the estuary. It was a long walk, what with the midday sun and our heavy loads, but eventually we reached the road and there, just as Paddy had said, was the gap in the hedge. Below the gap, the stepped ledges of Conger Rock ran for almost 100 yards at the foot of a steep grassy bank. To our right was the village of Kinsale; opposite, across the estuary, the angling centre and the tree-lined Bandon River valley. To our left the river led to the open sea and we felt that there could not be a more attractive or fishier-looking place anywhere.

We were all alone, and with that feverish haste that usually affects anglers in strange locales we began to tackle up. I was using a long, hollow glass beach rod with a heavy-duty fixed-spool reel loaded with 200 yards of 25 lb breaking strain (b.s.) nylon line. My terminal tackle was, I thought, quite suitable: a blood loop 18 inches above a 2 oz bomb, with a 12-inch trace of a 70 lb b.s. line with a 6/0 hook attached. Looking back now, how I wish I had done a little research on how to fish for Conger and not stuck to my own Yorkshire coast ideas. But this, I suppose, is the fascination of angling, and it is by our mistakes and omissions that we learn. It was by now one and a half hours before high water and this, according to Paddy, was the time to expect anything.

Tally, as usual, was first away, his typical Yorkshire outfit, Scarborough reel, greenheart rod, heavy nylon line, the large skelp of Mackerel and flat 6 oz lead, curling away in a practiced arc to plop, as Paddy had said, just 20 yards out. John, fishing with a set-up similar to my own, quickly followed, and finally I too was ready. With a large, bloody fillet of Mackerel dangling temptingly from the 6/0 hook, a gentle flick and it, too, was in the river.

I had moved 60 yards further upstream from my friends, more towards the town, and here I found an ideal spot. Two iron marlin spikes were set out in the flat rock so as to provide an ideal rod support. I laid the rod out, its tip projecting over the edge of the scar, the butt laid in between the two spikes, and began the wait.

The fresh wind had by now lapsed to a light breeze and with this cooling balm to our bodies we sank back into the grassy bank, lit our cigarettes and began to watch our hypnotic rod tips. As it happened, Tally was the first to get into something. His propped-up rod gently nodded, the line tightening so very slowly. It was soon over, for what real chance had a 6 lb dogfish in clear unobstructed water against such tackle? It was a start, anyway, in fact the only bite we had the first hour; but it was not high water yet and we were still hopeful.

So hot had the day become that I felt more like taking a nap than undergoing the possible exertions of hauling congers out of the dark, dank, limpid river that sluggishly curled past my feet. It was in this drowsy state that I suddenly saw my rod butt leap in the air, the tip dipping deeply down to the water below, the slipping clutch screaming in protest. With trembling hands and highly palpitating heart, I clumsily got the rod out of the supports and swept the tip high in the air, feeling as I did the surging thump of a heavy fish. For all of what seemed an eternity, but which could have been no more than a couple of minutes, I held on to a rod that was alive in my hands. There was little I could do except to try, unsuccessfully, to recover what line had been stripped from my reel in the mad plunge to the river bed. It must tire soon, and then I'd have him, a fish that would make these long days of saving so worthwhile, and not only that, it was certain to beat my best fish ever from the shore, a Codling of 6 lb 5 oz. It was with this supreme thought in my mind that I began to try and gain control and to pump whatever it was that had so decisively taken my bait away from the river bed.

I might well have tried to stop an irresistible force with an immovable object! The inevitable happened, although at the time it came as a violent disappointment: the line went slack. Whatever had been there had decided to go its own way and I had been unable to stop it. I reeled in, my heart at a very low ebb, to see exactly what had gone wrong. As I lifted the trace out of the water I saw that the hook had gone, the trace dangling limply like a straw in the wind. I put down the rod and carefully began to inspect the hook trace. The end was badly frayed and ragged; the hook had been bitten off! Seventy pounds breaking strain nylon line bitten through!

I sank back on to the bank, fumbling for a cigarette, and briefly told John and Tally what had happened. They were sympathetic and urged me to get straight back in and try again. I gazed at the frayed nylon and pondered. Could it have been due to the hook having been badly whipped on in the first place? No, that line had been bitten through and that was that. Anyway it wasn't the first fish I'd lost and it wouldn't be the last. It wasn't. In fact from the next four casts exactly the same thing happened. That sucking, plucking type of bite, the irresistible moving force, the madly alive rod and the usual ending: the trace bitten through.

At the end of 40 minutes I was furious, frustrated and disappointed. In all this time Tally and John had not had a touch but had just sat and watched the apparent amateur antics of five casts, five big fish and then five lost fish. John walked over and in words of one syllable asked why I had been unable to land them. I told him the story and to prove the point showed him the badly frayed and ragged trace end.

'You know,' he said, 'I think I have got a piece of wire in my strawbag. Do you mind if I have a cast from here?'

'No,' I replied, though I badly envied him that wire. He was soon back, a large skelp of Mackerel in one hand, the wire and a large 6/0 hook in the other. It was the most ineffective-looking trace I had ever seen in my life, but it might just work. On went the large fillet of

Mackerel and then out it went to plop into the now tide-assisted river. It was ten minutes before anything happened and we were, in fact, beginning to wonder whether the fishing was over now that the tide was beginning to ebb. Suddenly, just as before, the rod tip twitched, nodded, and then in one nerve-shattering movement the butt leapt upwards and the line began to peel off against the scream of the clutch. Quickly John grabbed the rod, struck hard, the rod tip arching swiftly into a graceful bow against the blue sky. John hung on grimly as the rod began to buck and shake, and I, now wild with excitement, began to shout at John: 'Be sure to keep its head up!' Slowly the line began to come, John pumping hard. Applying as much strain as the tackle would allow, he began to get control and, more important, it looked as though the wire was going to hold.

If I have ever willed a fish to be landed I willed that one. I prayed for that slender piece of wire to hold. Then almost at our feet through the now fast-flowing river came a barely discernible shape which with each turn of the reel became the unmistakeable lines of a conger. Long, black-backed, dark to grey-flanked, white-bellied, a twisting, cavorting, thrashing mass of eel finally came to the scar's edge.

'Where's the gaff?' yelled John frantically.

'We haven't got one!' replied Tally. 'We can land it without a gaff.'

As John backed away from the scar's edge, keeping the tip high and the line tight I reached over, grabbed the line and with an almighty heave hauled the strongly resisting eel on to the scar. Its antics did not diminish on its parting from its natural environment, and all hell was let loose as we tried to grab it on that narrow strip of grass and rock. But eventually we did pin it down and, as we had learnt in the boats, finally dispatched it. We sank back on to the grassy bank, not saying much, took out our cigarettes and began to take stock of what it was that had caused so much havoc: a conger, just under 5½ feet long, weighing 20 lb – not a giant by any standards, but to us it was the biggest fish we had seen caught from the shore, and one not easily forgotten.

'If only our coast offered fishing like this,' said Tally with feeling, as he carefully removed the hook and looked at the small piece of wire that had done its work so well.

'Come on, let's go and buy Paddy a deserved pint. There'll be no more fish now.'

'Ay,' said John.

He was right. The tide was now ebbing fast and the thought of that cool, golden pint at Dempsey's was a spur to our departure. And anyway, weren't we going Bass fishing in the morning?

Return to Ireland

It was six years later that we returned to Ireland, and this time there were three of us: Tally, Dave Johnson on his first trip, and myself. But this time the wondrous weather of 1962 did not materialise. The trip was to be in two parts: primarily week one was to be based in Westport, County Mayo to savour the fishing of Clew Bay as well as Achill Island and Belmullet; the second week was to be Bass fishing in County Kerry – very ambitious but we lived in hopes.

We had booked into a pub this time, the Angler's Rest, with Mine Host a Mr Gill. Apart from a chance meeting in the pub on the first Saturday of the holiday with three local heroes of the Easter Uprising of 1916, with an attendant crowd of about 20 locals, which turned out to be very memorable indeed, the only other real memory of that first week was the Belmullet Fishing Festival.

That I had ever heard of Belmullet was due entirely to *Angling* magazine and Clive Gammon's visit there. As a result of reading the article I wrote to a Father Moore, the Priest at Belmullet, who had much to do with the Fishing Festival organisation. He helped in every way possible and on the first Sunday of our holiday we drove from Westport on a lovely late August Sunday morning, to be greeted on arrival like long-lost family members; nothing was too much trouble. We had been allocated a family fishing boat, a 30-foot ex ship's lifeboat, so that there were just six of us in the boat: the three of us and the boat's skipper and his two grandchildren.

Belmullet sits on Blacksod Bay to the west and south of Belmullet, and Broadhaven Bay to the north and east of the village. We were to fish Blacksod Bay, which we did but with not as much success as we had hoped. In the event Tally won the 'Visitor's Cup' for a catch of 80-odd pounds of fish, whilst David and I both struggled to reach 40 lb apiece. The champion of the day took an incredible 456 lb of Tope! Bearing in mind that this was a very petite lady, such a catch was formidable. To land a Tope of any size (big ones run to 70 lb, the more modest to 45 lb or so), they never stop running hard and fighting every yard of their retrieval so you know you have been in a fight afterwards. The lady looked exhausted as well as quite sunburnt, and it must be said that I am as sure as I can be that there was no jiggery-pokery involved in her day's catch.

The very sad thing about the day was that apart from the white fish caught (Pollack, Coalfish, Cod, etcetera) everything else was dumped in a pile at the end of the pier. There must have been more than a ton of dead fish in that pile: Conger, Tope and Dogfish predominantly. I have always lived in the hopes that it was all collected and used on the land, but how they were to achieve that I have not got a clue; yet another huge and wasteful pile of fish that would otherwise have continued to give sport to anglers for many years yet to come.

The evening was spent in a thoroughly enjoyable get-together of club officials, participants and locals alike in the local schoolhouse, presided over by the indomitable Father Moore. On arrival back in Westport after that long drive from Belmullet we were, to say the very least, knackered.

It had been suggested to us during the Sunday evening celebrations that we should try and fish Blacksod Bay again before we made our way south to County Kerry and its Bass fishing. This was an offer we were delighted to receive, and accepted with alacrity.

Unfortunately by teatime on Monday the weather had begun to change and 24 hours later we had a south-westerly gale force 8 pushing force 9 and with heavy rain. We rang our contact in Belmullet who said we would not be able to fish Blacksod Bay, as we had much hoped, but Broadhaven would be fine as it was a sheltered bay.

Wednesday dawned with the gale still blowing, but the heavy rain had eased and now fierce showers lashed the area. This book is supposed to relate my fishing experiences but sometimes there were connected events or images that were of themselves memorable. The road out of Belmullet that eventually takes you to the access road to Broadhaven Bay was a winding road that climbed gently as it made its way north-eastwards. As we came to one particular stretch of meandering road, the sun appeared just for a few moments and lit the road ahead of us as if in a spotlight. Cycling up this road was a member of the Garda. This officer was very tall and thin, his official cap held in place by the head strap pulled tight under his chin, struggling desperately against both the hill and the gale-force wind. From his efforts it was clearly very hard work. The bike looked to my eyes like the bicycle that Jaques Tati had used in his film *Jour de Fete*. Anyone who remembers this film will recall Tati's encounter with a swarm of bees as he, the village postman, cycled his way through leafy lanes en route to delivering the post; hilarious does not come near it! Well, just like Tati's bike, the Garda's bike was a big-wheeled Victorian model and heavy with it, a model where the handlebars sit very close to the frame, so that as the Garda lifted his legs they all but crashed into the handlebars, and this difficulty was made even more of a problem as he struggled on his route. How he kept going and stayed upright … It was wondrous to watch, and pure Tati.

We had to stop the Garda because he was on his way to the weekly signing on of the local unemployed at the schoolhouse in Barnattra, some way ahead of us. In fact our boatman for the day, who lived on the south-eastern shore of the bay, was in this queue waiting to sign on. Since the queue was 200 yards long our host's concern was that we had to find him in that queue, get him to the front of it and then get him signed on. As we waited in the warmth and dry of our car, there before us was the long line of men, all waiting patiently as the winds blew and the showers swept over them. The Garda was as good as his word, and Eamon was brought out and ran to the front to sign on, then he ran over to the car and squeezed himself in. As we drove away, to our amazement, cheering broke out among the members of the queue and hands were raised to wave goodbye.

As before, our boat for the day was an ex ship's lifeboat, but this time it was moored 80 yards off the shingle and rocky beach. To get to our boat meant shipping out to it by means of Eamon's curragh with two broom handles as paddles, and to add to the fun it was a lee shore and the wind, if anything, had increased since we left the hotel. For anyone who does know what a curragh, is let me try and explain: about 16 feet long, no more than 24 inches wide, if that, and sitting as it does on the water its freeboard above the water is about 6 inches tops. The trick was to kneel in it and use the poles judiciously and make every pull of that broom handle count.

Tally and I went first with our tackle; the onshore waves were not that high, thank goodness, but they were bad enough and I was much relieved as we came alongside the ship's lifeboat. I wonder if that gunnel has ever been so hard-gripped as it was that morning. Once the gear was aboard Tally stayed in the boat whilst I returned to shore and brought David, who I then left in the boat with Tally whilst I returned to shore to get Eamon and our Belmullet host.

To our surprise Broadhaven Bay was surprisingly calm; however the nearer we came to the mouth of the bay the more came the lift and roll of the open Atlantic Ocean. We had come to the mouth of the bay to catch Mackerel, which was to be our bait for the day. The trouble was, they were few and far apart. To our left was the famous Erris Head, where a small lighthouse stood on the very corner of the bay's entry. Eamon brought the boat tight over to the rock edge that flanked the lighthouse and held it with the engine against the lift and fall of the broken water pouring into the bay from the open sea beyond. We were feathering for the Mackerel: I had a trace of six brightly coloured feather lures above a 6 oz lead, I reeled my trace up and yet again not a fish, and then I released the pressure on the reel and let the lead drop. After no more that a dozen revolutions of the reel spool the lead stopped. I had not noticed that in my concentration on keeping my trace line taught, Eamon had brought the boat even closer to the rock's edge. I looked up and saw how close we were to the grassy sward that ran between the lighthouse and the sea at its foot. Then I looked over the side of the boat. There, laid upon a pock-marked flat scar of rock, was my trace. Ye gods, we'll be aground! The bottom of the boat did scrape for just a moment, and then a wave lifted us and took us out and away from the scar's edge. 'How close was that to disaster?' I wondered, but before I had time to let the thought settle I lifted the rod tip and the lead came off the flattened rock and dropped into deep water.

The line came light! That has to be … Yes! Mackerel! They must have been tight against the face of the rock edge and Eamon must have known that from previous trips in search of bait.

Soon we had enough, probably about a couple of dozen, and with that we made our way back into the bay itself. We fished for about four hours by which time we were wet to the bone despite our wet gear, and cold with it. But it had been a good day: Common Skate, Thornback Skate, Conger Eels, Turbot, Flounders, the ubiquitous Dogfish. The fishing never for a moment stopped, and Dave took a Brill, which is rare enough to make any day memorable. We packed up and came back to the car in the same way we had got to the boat, and afterwards we were to our great surprise and pleasure wined and dined in the snug of a local pub, bringing to an end a memorable visit to Belmullet.

Then it was Kerry and the Bass. By the time we arrived at Dingle the weather seemed to stall and so our hopes rose. It was not to be, though: apart from a trip to the Blue Lagoon, a quite beautiful stretch of beach near the Banna Strand, north-east of Tralee, there was to be no more fishing.

We would never have found such a spot as this even had we had the time to search for such a place. We were taken there by the local Customs Officer, a keen sea and Bass angler who did everything in his power to help us; he had even gone out of his way to dig us some lugworm! Such kindness and hospitality that went beyond any call of duty was the norm when it came to our contact with locals in Eire.

We tried very hard to succeed at the Blue Lagoon but it was Tally who took our only Bass, a fish of about 3 lb which Tally returned to the sea. Even as we stood by the Blue Lagoon the clouds began to build, and as they grew and began to fill the whole sky, the wind started to freshen by the minute. By the time we got back to our base in Dingle it had started to rain as well as blow. Little did we know just how bad the weather was to come.

That evening the shipping forecast for 'Irish Sea, Shannon, Rockall, Malin...' was for gale force 8 increasing 9, 10 and 11. It was the first time I had heard the shipping forecast warn of a gale force 11; within days the shipping forecast gave winds to force 12. On one occasion we decided to drive out to Slea Head and we parked the car tight against the cliff face that flanked the road and towered above us. We could only get out of the car by opening the doors tight against the rock face, and to get to the parapet wall that flanked the roadway we had to get down on all fours and scramble across the road as best we could. Once against that parapet wall, there was some shelter from the screaming banshee of a gale.

The idea was to prepare your camera and then leap up and, pointing the camera in the direction of the shot you wanted, press the shutter and then get down behind the parapet wall as quickly as you could. Indeed the wind was so strong that I saw the wave tops being ripped from the waves themselves, so that it looked as if the sea itself was just a rolling carpet of heavy swells, giving the impression of a windless day. The ripped-off wave tops rose in spirals ever upwards throughout your field of vision to disappear into the grey, lowering, overcast sky above us. There was nowhere we could fish despite our looking hard for suitable places; we could hardly stand up, the wind was so severe. The weather that week was the worst I ever experienced, save the East Coast floods of 1952, memorable in every way – unless you wanted to go fishing.

We flew home two days early, hugely disappointed, and even though the weather had eased a fraction the flight was not without incident: screams and shouts of fear as the plane was thrown about the sky, with one passenger suffering a coronary that required an ambulance on arrival at Yeadon. It took four attempts to get the Viscount down before a successful landing was achieved.

A year later I was back, but this time with a different set of companions: Martin Scotter, Noddy Bannister and the inimitable Fred Hall. Again economics raised its ugly head and we went to Ireland with my estate car, a Morris 1300, and travelled via the Stranraer–Larne ferry. Looking back now, despite the modest successful fishing we all enjoyed, there was one overriding incident that all but spoilt the whole holiday. The Irish Troubles were very much on the boil that year, 1969. We had talked about the problems and how it might effect us, but so great was the thought of Ireland and its Bass fishing that we decided to go regardless.

We arrived on the outskirts of Belfast just on dusk and it was probably the ensuing darkness that brought about a mistake in the direction we took. As we were going along a relatively busy but darkened road – we were later told it was the Falls Road – we came to a well-lit crossroads. On one corner there was a public house with a roll of concertina'd barbed wire laid upon the pavement by its doorway, and on two of the other corners were small groups of men.

I instinctively slowed the car down as we approached the crossroads, looking for road signs to help us get on our way. Then suddenly from out of the darkness to our right came an armed soldier who flagged us down. I stopped the car within 50 yards of the crossroads and the soldier, a Corporal, approached the car with what appeared to be a submachine gun at the ready. The euphoria in the car died almost immediately and questions flew at me, none of which I tried to answer.

I wound down the car window. 'Good evening, Corporal,' I said, with as much confidence as I could muster, which was not very much.

'You! Out of the car! Now!'

I got out as fast as I was able, heart in mouth, and stood still.

'Getcha 'ands on the car roof and spread yer legs wide. Now!'

I obeyed. At that moment there broke out shouts and yells from the crossroads and I turned to look. The noise was coming from a group of people who were shouting at each other. I could not make out what was being said.

'Keep yer 'ead still and don't move, yer 'ear me?'

'Yes, Corporal.'

The Corporal now turned on his large torch and flashed it into the car, the light falling upon each of my friends, who sat there wide-eyed and in utter silence.

'What yer doin' 'ere?' he asked as his torch took in the rods in their protective tubing on the roof rack.

Even as he asked it, I realised that to anyone in these circumstances a car with a roof rack full of long thin tubes and the like must have been extemely suspicious.

'We're trying to get to Newry. We are on our way to a fishing holiday in Kerry.' In saying it, this simple sentence struck me as ridiculous in the extreme, but there it was, it was the truth.

'Yer what? Goin' fishing?' His scepticism was understandable. He lifted the Sten gun and the torch, and shone the light directly into my eyes.

'Corporal, we are four Yorkshiremen going to Kerry for a sea fishing holiday. Those tubes hold our fishing rods and those bulky bags contain potato forks to dig our bait!'

He swore harshly under his breath.

'What the **** are yer doin' 'ere, on this road? Yer on t' wrong road.'

'We must have missed the right road. I don't know what else I can say, but we are who I say we are, and you can check our hotel in Newry if you wish.'

At that moment there came a lot of noise from within the public house.

'Just do not move, OK?' said the Corporal.

'I won't.'

The Corporal made his way across the road to where a small group of soldiers were standing watching, and he spoke to someone, but I could not hear what was said. A few moments later he returned.

'You see the road ahead of you?'

'Yes,' I replied.

'Get in that car and drive straight down that road. Get the 'ell out of 'ere and don't stop, yer 'ear me?'

'Yes, Corporal.'

I got in the car and within seconds we were off, as fast as I dared drive, across the crossroads and down the road. The groups of people who had stood watching us had somehow disappeared. Never was I more relieved to get away from anywhere than I was that night in Belfast. Yet the night was not yet over. We had to get to Newry, and we were already very late.

It was gone eleven as I drove into the Ardmore Hotel car park, and much relieved at our safe arrival made my way up the entrance steps to the Reception. Our arrival was to say the very least coolly received, and when I asked if we were too late for a meal I was put right in my place.

'The dining room closed at nine-thirty. Sir, we're sorry, but its much too late I am afraid. The chef and his staff have gone now.'

'Just a cotton-picking minute,' I retorted. 'It's not our fault we are so late. We got held up by the Army in a place called the Falls Road, and that plus all the rest of the hold-ups in getting through Belfast is why we are late getting here.' I was getting angrier by the moment.

'Say again, sir?' said the receptionist.

I explained again and added that we had not enjoyed the experience of having a Sten gun pointed at us and all but pushed into my mouth. The receptionist quickly disappeared and duly returned with someone who was obviously the hotel manager.

'We do apologise, sir, for your unpleasant experience in Belfast. It's a sign of these difficult times I am afraid. But if you will get your friends and your luggage into the hotel we will do all we can to make up for what has happened.'

And they did, and in spades. It was well after half past one in the morning before we got to bed, all appetites more than satisfied and a very great deal happier than when we had arrived.

Within two years of our visit to this fine hotel, it was destroyed by an IRA bomb.

The first part of our holiday was to be spent in Kinsale. This time we stayed at Acton's Hotel and we enjoyed every minute. We went boat fishing and took Pollack predominantly, with fish up to 12 lb but nothing particularly memorable. Then came the real purpose of our trip: to fish for Bass in County Kerry. It is very easy nowadays to look upon our trip as if we were a bunch of naive amateurs, but – and it is a very big but – Bass fishing for the vast majority of sea anglers in the UK, and Europe for that matter, was very much a mystery, and fishing in Ireland for Bass was in its very early days. Visiting anglers relied very much upon reports in the UK angling press and it was on these sources that our holiday had been based.

The Irish Government had set up the Ireland Fisheries Trust (IFT) and it was very helpful indeed, but although it catered for sea angling, its main target was the coarse angling, and coarse anglers especially in the UK; thus we more or less ignored whatever information the IFT had for County Kerry and its Bass fishing.

What follows is how that fishing was recorded by myself at the time in my diary:

Wednesday, 8th October
Stradbally. Fishing either side of stream entry onto the beach. State of tide: half flood tide. Gale force 8/9 southerly, with excellent surf; weather, overcast.
Martin: three Bass (one 5¾ lb, one 2¾ lb, one schoolie Bass) all taken on legered black lugworm.

Thursday, 9th October
Stradbally, as yesterday.
State of tide: two hours before high water. South-easterly wind force 5/6, with excellent surf (water very clear); weather, bright, cloudy.
Fred: one Bass – 5¾ lb.
Nav: one Bass – 6½ lb.
Fish taken on legered black lugworm.

Friday, 10th October
Fishing from rock ledges on Slea Head.
State of tide: Just before and after high water. A beautiful, glorious and hot cloudless day.

Dogfish, Conger Eels, Mackerel and a monstrous Bull Huss lost at our feet.

Nav took a Bass of 2¾ pounds on ABU Koster lure.

Martin lost a very good Bass from the same shoal as mine had come from.

Saturday, 11th October

Stradbally as before.

State of tide: two hours after high water. Easterly wind. Very hot and sunny. The sea was gin clear.

Nav: one Bass – 2 lb exactly. Fish taken on legered black lugworm.

Tuesday, 14th October

Stradbally as before.

State of Tide: two hours after high water. South-westerly gale 7/8, slight surf, grey overcast; water very clear.

Martin: two Bass each exactly 2 lb.

Fred: one Bass of 2 lb.

Nav: one Bass of 2 lb.

What is interesting is that our bait was black lugworm, no Mackerel strip nor 'Joey Mackerel', no soft crab or 'peelers', all first-class Bass baits but not tried by us. No thought was given to any other type of bait, which in retrospect was somewhat stupid, but that was how our minds worked in those days.

The digging of black lugworm is always a problem in Ireland in that there are not many places where you can go and dig the worms, bearing in mind that the lugworm you want is not the soft and readily breakable 'blasties', but what is referred to nowadays as 'yellowtails'. These are the very best of lugworm; they stay on the hook for the majority of casting techniques (well, almost!) and fish all the time they are in the water. The problem is finding a beach that holds yellowtails or even the better quality 'blast' lugworm. But then, of course, having found such a beach you have to be able to dig them, which is a very great deal easier said than done.

Bass fishing: it was an exciting, mysterious prospect to us. You must remember that we were all working young men: Noddy a joiner, Fred a painter and decorator, Martin a TV engineer, and myself a professional quantity surveyor. For all of us work came first, for me very much so as my work responsibilities had grown enormously after 12 years of effort. Thus, opportunities to go fishing were grabbed at with both hands, and an annual holiday even more so. Ireland was then as now Nirvana, Shangri-La, the land of dreams for us, and over the years that I – we – visited Ireland it had proved this.

When we came over the Connor Pass that first morning en route to Stradbally and looked down on to the strand below us, the excitement in that car was palpable. Conversations were brief: the odd phrase, questions that we already knew the answer to, or that we could not as yet answer.

Stradbally is situated on the north side of the Dingle Peninsula, it sits more or less in the middle of the peninsula on Brandon Bay. To see it as we did for the first time that Wednesday morning in early October really took our breath away, despite the fact that we all came from a seaside resort and were at the seaside every chance we got. There was a southerly gale blowing, from land to sea, which we ignored; there was no chance of anything (within reason!) spoiling this day.

It was low water when we arrived, the breaking surf white-fringed against a shade of green that was not quite emerald green. After the drab grey, blue-black and browns of our native North Sea, the colour of the sea in Brandon Bay was a sight to behold. The breaking surf was high: each breaking wave about 8 feet high, the wave rose from a dark line of shadow, to climb, then curl and fall with force into a line of white that disappeared almost as quickly as it appeared, the once high wave now a table of water, foam-flecked, and running with force to the beach where we stood in silence watching. From us to the first line of breaking surf was about 130 yards, each table of moving water coming in to the beach about 40 yards wide.

To fish for Bass upon such a storm beach is in my view just about the pinnacle of the sport of beach fishing anywhere. For some anglers this level of fishing is achieved with Bone Fish in the Bahamas, Florida Keys or Mauritius, or wherever. For others it may be big game fishing from a boat, with Marlin or Tuna or even Conger Eels their quarry. For me and my three companions that morning, it is a storm beach and Bass. I was so impressed by my surroundings that morning, that when we walked across the beach I said to Martin that when I bought my own home I would call it 'Stradbally', and so I did.

I stood at the sea's edge and looked about me; it was impossible to look for those signs that would give me an idea as to what the seabed was like. When 'Cod bashing', our usual quarry, you are always looking for those signs that indicate that there is a hole or merely a depression in the seabed, a drop in sand level that could hold fish against the run of the tide. The signs you look for are a fall-off in wave height as it approaches the shore; that fall-off in height tells you that where the wave fell off there is a hole or depression directly beneath.

I looked at the beach to my left, right and behind me. It was very, very flat and the tables of water before me gave no indication that there were any holes on this beach whatever. Looking at how far out the breaking waves were, I wondered if I could cast far enough to get beyond the outside line of surf and quickly realised that I could not; but I could get reasonably close, or so I thought. It was then I remembered an article by Clive Gammon that said that there are times when the Bass may well be between you, the angler standing thigh-deep in the surf, and the shore itself, so casting far off was not an issue: the Bass could be anywhere in this surf in their search for food.

So, just how do you start? For me it was inevitable that I would try and cast out as far as I could; that was what you did when 'Cod bashing', my usual prey. I waded out until the table of water was just over knee-high and then I cast as hard and as well as I could. The rod, a Hardy Longbow; an ABU Ambassadeur 9000 reel, a 5 oz lead, with single 4/0 Cannelle hook on an 18-inch trace, baited with a good-sized black lugworm. I turned my back to the surf, pushed the rod tip away from me, the lead swinging out in an arc. Let it go. It reaches the end of its arc and starts to come back towards you. Wait! Let the lead come almost to your shoulder, then just as it stops in its arc and starts to go back whence it came. You begin to turn and pull the lead around, pull hard now, swivel your body, feel the compression. Hit it! The lead flew high and about 90 yards long and I was well pleased. The tide was now making and soon I was making my way back towards the beach, trying very hard to keep a degree of tension in my 18 lb b.s. line, waiting all the time for that touch, pluck or direct yank of a bite that for me, that day, never arrived.

Every Bass I have ever caught has never bitten in what is a supposedly conventional way, whatever that is! The bite when it came almost always caught me by surprise, and upon the strike it was always as if I had hooked a very solid object that was not in the position I believed it to be. By the time I had realised that I had hooked a Bass, the fish would be quickly moving one way or another, and I had to reel quickly to maintain a tight line. Thus, slack line bites were almost always the most difficult to hit.

The moment you feel contact, your rod as you sweep it up and back stops as if it has hit a wall, then the tip curves forward, the rod now alive, shaking in your hands ... this is worth all the efforts made, all those moments of disappointment now forgotten. Afterwards it seems as if the fight lasted minutes but in truth it does not last long. Your heart in your mouth, you look into the moving surf for a glimpse, the flash of silver; it is fleeting, momentary, then it has disappeared again. The line tight, you are breathless and shaking all over! And then it is at your feet or pushed past you by a wave, and then you try to scoop it up and it is in your arms or on your fingertips! A Bass! It may be a 'schoolie', or the best you've ever taken; but for me a Bass is a Bass – is fantastic!

It is hard work, tiring, surf fishing. The casting, be it long or short; the look-out for the odd rogue wave; and when standing in silence waiting for that bite, your concentration is absolute. It is in that concentration that the most effort is made and your energy seeps away. You notice the gannets, feeding just beyond the breaking waveline, their dives, the splash of their hitting the sea, their bedraggled escape, flying away with or without their prize. You notice everything and anything that points towards evidence of fish being present, but such observation can break that all-important concentration.

But that first day was Martin's day. We had caught our first Bass and we had another nine days yet to come. It could only get better, and it did. By the end of the holiday we had taken a total of 35 lb of Bass, the best a fish of 6½ lbs to me at Stradbally; nothing like our hopes, but we had caught Bass and that had been the purpose of the exercise.

Twelve months later my life had changed irrevocably; I had bought a house and called it, as I had promised myself, 'Stradbally'. I had also got engaged to Julie (we married in 1971) and this fact added to an even more responsible work load really began to interfere with my fishing life. However, in October 1970, four of us returned to County Kerry, but this time to Waterville on the Ring of Kerry. The four included John and Fred as before, and we were joined by a new visitor to Ireland, Ian Parrish, with myself making up the four.

Early in 1970 the *Angling Times* ran an article on Waterville, concentrating on a hotelier called Mr Abbey Hoggard who ran the Bay View Hotel on Waterville's seafront, and the Bass fishing the area provided. This article was the trigger to returning to Ireland and Kerry.

I made enquiries during the spring of 1970 and after a discussion between the four of us it was agreed that come October of that year we would go to Waterville and the Ring of Kerry and have another go for the Bass. We stayed at the Bay View Hotel and it proved to be everything we had hoped it would be: good food, comfortable, and helpful in everything that we wanted to do or visit. But probably most important of all was that Abbey Hoggard, Mine Host, was an angler and helped us as to where to go and the availability of bait. This was invaluable.

Essentially, the two weeks of our stay fell into three parts: we began at Derrynane, went rock fishing off Valentia Island, and had the token day's boat fishing out of Cahersiveen. Derrynane Beach was reached after a 6-mile drive, on the Ring of Kerry itself, south from Waterville heading to Caherdaniel, then leaving the main road and driving down to a public car park set midst some beautiful woodland. Through the trees behind us was home of the Irish patriot known as 'The Liberator', Daniel O'Connell; before us were sand dunes; and between these and Derrynane Bay away to our right was Derrynane Beach. There was no one to be seen that first morning and so it proved for the rest of that week, ideal for our purposes. From the top of the sand dunes the beach was about 500 yards long and ended with a gap in the dunes 50 yards wide that gave the sea access to a lagoon that separated the beach and sand dunes from the mainland beyond. The beach was quite steep, about 70 yards wide, then it flattened off to the beach proper which was then exposed for 30 yards of flat sand.

We were to discover as the week wore on that to spin from the beach where the flooding tide entered the lagoon that lay behind the dunes was a great spot for Bass. Stradbally was a lovely place, but it must be said that Derrynane was just as beautiful if not more so. The steepish beach was much like our favourite beaches on Holderness and in every way we all felt very much at home.

What follows is what I recorded at the time:

Monday, 12th October
Derrynane Beach, a steepish sand beach overlooking a small bay.
State of tide: half flood tide, next to no wind, overcast, moderate surf.
Fred: three Bass (one of 8 lb, one of 5 lb and one of 4 lb) all taken on legered black lugworm.

Tuesday, 13th October
Derrynane Beach, conditions as Monday, except tide an hour later.

Fred: one Bass (4 lb).
Ian: one Bass (7 lb).
Nav: one Bass (6½ lb).

Wednesday, 14th October
Derrynane Beach, grey overcast, rain, except tide an hour
later.
John: two Bass (one of 9 lb, and a 'schoolie')
Fred: one Bass (3 lb; taken spinning at end of beach/inlet to
lagoon).
Nav: one Bass, a 'schoolie'.

Then the weather changed: the wind moved from south to south-easterly then to the east, for us a disaster, for with the change of wind direction the sea flattened off. The Bass disappeared and we had to do something else.

That something else was boat fishing. Ian was desperately keen to catch a big Skate so it was agreed that we'd give it a go, and so on a lovely sunny morning we set off from Cahersiveen bound for Valentia Island. As before, our boat was an ex ship's lifeboat, some 30 feet long, double-ended. This particular boat was used throughout the summer to catch Mackerel commercially.

That morning we first had to get bait, the ubiquitous Mackerel. We sailed for about 30 minutes until we were two-thirds of the way along the length of Valentia Island's north flank. There is a headland, which from the sea is all but disguised as part of the rocky cliffs, that looks much like another, but this headland is special. Beennakryraka Head it is called, and locals have fished for centuries from the high flat scar that marks out this headland.

Engine off and coming to a drift about 100 yards from the headland, down went our feathered traces. The lures got no further than 30 or 40 feet below the surface then the line went slack then pulled sharply, and six Mackerel were up and in a fish box as quick as that. All five of us took Mackerel and within five minutes we had enough bait for a week's boat fishing let alone a day. This area of sea was alive, thick, with Mackerel. I had never seen so many, nor signs of so many Mackerel in all my fishing life. It was quite a place. We decided there and then that come what may we would find this spot on Valentia Island and fish it. The name of it, Beennakryraka Head was, long as it sounded, memorable; at least it was after the four of us had repeated it several times.

The boat trip was a disaster of sorts in that we wasted two and a half hours fishing for Ian's Skate with ne'r a bite to the rest of us. Then our boatman quietly said to me that 400 yards from where we were wasting our time was an underwater reef that offered some great fishing. Were we interested? The next two hours are lost to memory now, save John's 14 lb Cod, Pollack up to 14 lb, fishing that never stopped for moment. It was probably one of the best day's boat fishing I have ever had, and a day that would otherwise have been lost was saved. We sailed for home very satisfied.

So, the weather unchanging, with easterly winds continuing, we decided to find Beennakryraka Head. In doing so we broke the law, quite inadvertently I must add, by being one of the very first members of the public to drive across the newly built bridge at Portmagee! Once across the bridge it was just a matter of following the road up the hill, past the school, all the time looking away to our left for a recognisable point on the coastline that we had seen from the boat. Then we saw it: a stream, and by the cliff's edge, some standing stones. We unloaded the car and set off to follow the stream and after a good hike found a worn path through the cliffs that led down onto a large flat area of rocky scar set 30 feet above the sea.

We had only just arrived when the boat we had spent the previous day in arrived off the headland, and our boatman and his mate (who had not been with us in the boat) began 'jigging', using hand lines with 12-hook Mackerel traces attached. And catch them they did, three fish on one drop, then seven or eight the next, and more often than not 12 struggling Mackerel would be lifted quickly up into a rapidly filling boat. They fished in this manner for most of the rest of the day, moving the boat off and away from the rock face after each drift; they had to move off to avoid possible disaster by collision with the rock face.

By late afternoon, the gunnels of the boat sat deep, close to the surface of the sea, its load of caught Mackerel making its movement ugly, sloppy. Had any kind of lifting sea appeared, the boat would have been in jeopardy of capsizing. But the calm remained and the boat set off for Cahersiveen late that afternoon, its work done.

The rock fishing was brilliant. There was 90 feet of water at low tide and around 120 feet at high water, which was a new experience to us. Fishing off this rocky point was without a doubt the best rock fishing I have ever experienced anywhere. Cod, Pollack, Conger Eels, Spur Dogs, Bull Huss, Smooth Hound, and if you could get your lure or baited hook through the myriad shoals of Mackerel, there were Bass, Tope and Sharks of all kinds. It was quite amazing. This place had been fished for generations and when some locals turned up they began to fish with orange Corlene lines, baited feathers and a stone more often than not as a sinker. They did quite well, but we took a great many more fish, our tackle being that more sophisticated, and everything we took that was edible we gave to them. Fantastic fishing!

In 1976, myself and two friends returned to fish this point after a break of six years. It was as desolate as the Sahara Desert; in the ten hours we were there we caught one Mackerel, and the three of us had tried all day to catch Mackerel for our bait. Yes, we caught a Conger Eel and some Dogfish but little else.

What could have happened? It broke my heart. Having told all our angling friends of this wondrous spot, to find it as we did was a huge, huge disappointment. Then, after making enquiries locally it transpired that deepwater trawlers complete with their factory ships (French and Spanish, East European Soviet bloc nations, and so on) had arrived in the early summer of 1972, with the inevitable consequences. Heaven only knows what quantities of Mackerel had been taken over the years, let alone all those fish that would have been there as well as the Mackerel. Even now, all these years later, it still hurts, and my blood pressure goes through the roof just thinking about it. Just how stupid are we anglers to have allowed this wholesale destruction of what was once a fishery of wonder? A joy for generations now destroyed, probably for a very long time if not for all time.

A Taste of Irish Cream

'Pint of t' usual, Cora, and tha'd better take money for t'other two jars. The lads'll be in 'ere in a moment.'

'Coming right up now,' said Cora, her rich Irish brogue sweet on the ear.

Fred, his order now in, turned to survey the lounge bar, a large and very lush room, now utterly deserted this late October evening. He looked towards the door as John came marching in.

'Gorrem in, Fred?' he asked, his blue eyes sweeping the long bare bar.

'He has indeed,' interrupted Cora, lifting a large streaming pint of that dark succulent Irish cream onto the bar counter. 'Have you caught any of the Bass today?' asked Cora, her dark eyes looking appreciatively at the big men now leaning against the bar.

'Cora, my love,' John replied, 'whatever you do, don't ask!'

It was as bad as that. From the moment of our arrival the winds had been in the east, and with these easterlies had come a calm over the seas that flanked the rugged coast of County Kerry. No matter where we had travelled there had been no surf, and though the rock fishing was really out of this world, it was the Bass that we had come for. Time was passing too; we had one week of our fortnight's holiday left, and all the signs were that the area of high pressure over northern Scotland, and the deep depression over the Low Countries, were almost unmoving.

'I've been havin' a shufti at the map, lads,' I said, 'and what with tonight's shipping forecast, I think that I've found a spot of light in an otherwise black, black night.'

'Aye, like the patch of light I've found at the bottom of this glass. Come on, John, it's your round!' said a much-depressed Fred.

But there was a spot of light, a glimmer in the gloom. With the slow eastward passage of those areas of high and low pressure, and slow they certainly were, the wind was going to veer from the south-east where it had been for the last two days, to the south, and with it any south-facing beach was going to have its first surf in days.

'What's the time, Fred?' I asked.

'Supping time. It's ten to six, just gone.'

'Cora, love, your radio, please.'

'This won't make the wind blow any different,' said an amused Cora, passing over a somewhat battered transistor radio. A few quick twirls and one thump later there came through the depths of the ether a far and very distant voice.

'Thames... crackle ... hiss ... roar ... Biscay ... southerly ...' The sound again faded but we had heard that magic word 'south'; if only we could hear the rest. It came back, faintly at first, but getting stronger all the time:' Irish sea, Shannon ... southerly ... four to six', and now it was fading again, but we had heard enough.

'All right, Nav, what's so special about this place you've found?'

'Aye, come on and let's hear it, anything to relieve the disaster of this 'ere week. Where the 'ell is it?'

'Well, the map is a bit vague to say the least of it ...'

'What d'ye mean vague?' asked John. 'How the hell can a beach be vague?'

'Well, it is vague on this scale of map, but it does show a tiny strip of yellow between two headlands, and it also shows a bridge.'

'A bridge? Then there must be water, a stream or summat?'

'Aye, Fred, that's what made me excited.'

'Shades of Stradbally,' said John, almost under his breath. 'It sounds too good to be true!'

'It probably is, John, but we've got the bait.'

'I only used three baits today,' said Fred.

The morning dawned fine. It had been a wet night, in more senses than one, and there had been little chat at the breakfast table.

'Thar was right about t'wind; it is in t' south now an' all,' said Fred, carefully putting his beloved rod into the car.

'Aye, let's just hope that the wind that kept banging that flaming door all night has produced a surf of any size, just six inches high would be a bloody vast improvement,' said John irritably as he swung his long legs into a somewhat cramped front seat.

'John,' I said as I turned on the ignition, 'there must be some surf this morning. That wind must have been pushing force six at times last night, and if that forecast is anything to go by, it's been blowing southerly from as far away as the Bay of Biscay, so there must be some surf.'

We took the low road away from the hotel, a long, grey, wet ribbon of splattered tarmac that clearly indicated that it was much used by the makers of the famous Kerrygold butter, as they made their daily journey to the creamery. We did not have too far to go, 12 miles I reckoned, across some of the most magnificent scenery in Europe. According to the map we had to find a small right-hand turn-off 3 miles from the hotel, climb up the side of a mountain, and there on the other side, at the bottom of a long tree-lined valley, was (we hoped) the beach. We found the turn-off without much difficulty and followed a much narrower road that climbed it seemed ever upwards towards lowering grey clouds that gave the rugged hillside an almost bearded appearance. The road continued to climb, getting narrower with every yard, and with it the wild red fuchsia that flanked the road began to sweep the sides of the car, leaving behind us a long trail of fallen petals to litter the grey road. Suddenly, we reached the top, and turning hard to the right, found directly in front of us a view of sheer beauty. A long valley, not quite tree-lined, lay before us and, at its end, a few miles ahead, was a small beach set between two towering headlands.

'Hey, just look at that surf. Where the hell has that come from, eh?' asked a now awake and excited Fred.

It was superb. From far beyond the headland there rose with a patient regularity a long dark shadow that moved with purposeful pace towards the narrow strip of golden beach. As the leading edge of the wave hit the rugged headland away to our left, the wave reared up and broke with an emerald and white explosion of power that pushed the crystals of sharp white spray high up the rock face. The wave itself, apparently unchecked in its momentum, carried on to rise and break with that curl and roar that is typical of a storm beach surf in ideal conditions. Inside the surf, long, flat tables of water sped across the narrow, flat beach, curling and hissing around a series of long flat scars of rock that lay like broken driftwood down the beach.

'It's perfect. Absolutely perfect,' said John, looking at the line of breakers with knowing eyes.

We had now reached the bottom of the long valley road, and as the road turned to the left to run parallel to the beach, we found a large area of grass on which grazed a few fat sheep. We pulled the car off the road, and got out. It did not take us very long to unpack our gear. In such surroundings it would have been surprising if it had. It was not low water for another hour, and we had time to survey the beach properly, not that there was much to survey, for the beach was only 300 yards wide at the most!

Fred was first away, grabbing the bait bucket with a flourish and scrambling down the sand cliffs that separated the road from the beach. I quickly followed, my rod in my right hand, haversack half on and half off my left shoulder in the rush to get away. Fred had decided that our base for the coming day was going to be the rocky headland on our right. He had now reached it and was putting his gear on the shelves of rock that nature, the sea, and time had bludgeoned out of the lichen-covered rock strata. As I approached, he turned and looked at me, his dark brown eyes twinkling with the anticipation we all shared.

'What do y'reckon they call this place, Nav?'

'I believe it's called Noel Strand.'

'Noel Strand, eh? Well, it looks like the Bass beach of my dreams. If it lives up to its promise, I swear I will buy you that Black Velvet drink, champagne and all!'

So saying he turned and delved into the seaweed-filled bucket and extracted a long black lug that was, he hoped, the key to the magical

The author fishing 'Sherkin Strand' – Noel Strand in reality – Co. Kerry, Eire

kingdom. By now John too had arrived, and in the silence that prevailed, all was activity. The surf was quite big, but still not big enough to warrant our using our heavy surf poles, and so, armed with our light Bass sticks and the small Swedish multipliers that had added a new dimension to our fishing, we made our way to the sea's edge.

'We must use a degree of common sense, lads, fishing this place,' said John, looking at each of us in turn.

'You mean one to fish the stream, one to fish the middle, and one to fish this side, casting down alongside that scar of rock?' I replied.

'Aye, fair enough,' said Fred, 'I'll fish yon side, alongside that stream.'

'I'll take this side, John,' I said as I turned to walk the few yards to the sea's edge.

'OK,' said John, 'and tight lines.'

There was still a little time left to low water, and time to give the spot I had decided to fish a good looking over. I waded out slowly through the gin-clear water that came and surged around my ankles, and stood on the scar of rock that flanked the right-hand side of the beach. The scar was about 6 feet wide, and very rough, rising at least knee-high within its length as it ran from the top of the beach and disappeared into the sea. That could cause problems if I were fortunate enough to get into a good fish that decided to go for those rock edges; but it could be a major asset too, for those gullies and cracks would certainly hold a wealth of feed.

By now both Fred and John had begun to wade through the first table of surf, their rods held high across their chests, the water sweeping around their knees with sufficient force to make them have to lean forward to continue their walking progress. John, having the least distance to walk, had reached that point from which he thought he could cast easily to, he hoped, the waiting fish. He turned his back to the sea, the lead swinging away from the rod in a long gentle curve, the rod dipped and he began to pull it round, the rod beginning to compress under the combined efforts of both terminal gear and the applied power of his arms. Then the release, the rod unfolding along its whole length, its tip pointing to the far horizon, and the lead and bait flying in a long high arc to fall just in front of the rising first wave of the surf. Fred, too, had now cast and though it was not as long as John's cast, it was far enough. I watched them for a few minutes, and then I began to wade out alongside the scar. I had decided to put the bait out as far as I could and a little to my left, for what tide there was was moving from my left to the right. With the surf now almost thigh-deep, I pushed the Spindrift as hard as my leader would allow, and away the lead flew high, wide to the left, to fall inside the far-breaking comber. Now, we must wait.

I did not have to wait long. Suddenly there was a sharp pull, followed a second or two later by yet another sharp pull. I swept the rod back hard, and stepped backwards to help pick up any slack line. The rod arched over, but this was no hoped-for Bass. After a spirited battle there came towards me through the spume-surfaced water an enormous Flounder; it was as big as a meat plate, and thick with it. I reached into my anorak for my scales, and put the hooked ring gently under the gill case. The needle pointed at just under 2¾ lb, 8 ounces better than any 'butt' I'd ever caught before. I took the hook out of the corner of its mouth, the first time in a long time that any 'butt' I'd nailed was lip-hung! I slipped him back into his own world and he sped away seawards, obviously none the worse for his incursion into our alien world. As I rebaited I looked over towards John and Fred, but as yet they were unmoving. Having rebaited with a smaller lugworm than last time, I waded again down alongside the scar and punched the baited Cannelle into almost the same place as before.

The tide had now turned, and with its turn the wind increased a little. Along the top of the curling line of surf that rose 100 yards in front of me a lone gull skirted the front of the falling wave, its wings scarcely moving other than to lift either wing tip to take advantage of the updraught of air released from that tumult of breaking water. At the sea's edge both Oystercatchers and Dunlin walked together with staccato rhythm of short runs and head dipping that gives the birds a comic look. Small patches of weed, long torn from its sea bed by some earlier storm, drifted past, tendrils catching around my boots as they were swept first towards the shore and then seawards by each run and turn of wave.

Suddenly, my line fell slack, the line dropping from the rod tip to hang in a loose curve. It had almost taken me by surprise. I reacted with what seemed treacle arms; it seemed that I would never get the rod tip up high and back quickly enough. I ran backwards as fast as the depth of water and my beating heart would allow, cranking that small reel handle like one possessed. The line tightened in front of me, the rod arched over, and I hit it hard, the rod a live thing as it began to walk across my chest. I continued to back up towards the beach, watching the line that glinted in the watery yellow sunlight, trying to see just where the fish was and if at all possible to keep it away from that scar. It was some fish.

There was no moving the fish. The clutch whined with each charge, and instead of gaining line I was rapidly losing it. I dare not tighten the clutch too much, but I had to stop that fish taking any more line. I touched the star drag with my fingertips, easing the tips of the star even tighter; it seemed to make little difference. I began to walk towards the fish that was still going very hard seawards and began to pray that the 12 lb b.s. line would not break. It held, and I now began to pick up line, not a lot but enough to renew my hopes. Gently, slowly, the line came in, becoming easier with every turn, and my hopes now began to soar. Then, as if to remind me the battle was far from over, the tip was pulled down hard, viciously, forcing me to ease the pressure of the clutch. The fish was now about 40 yards in front of me, and I saw for a moment a long flank of silver suspended in the air as the fish leapt, to fall with an almighty splash in front of a fast-approaching run of surf. I now began to back up the beach, and as I did so the fish began to run hard to my right, straight towards the scar, and my heart sank. I ran stumbling to my left, trying very hard to keep the rod high, and the line tight. I prayed as I ran, the promises of a man in real need I made in those frantic moments, but that fish still kept going right. It was at that moment that I heard John's voice.

'Keep its bloody 'ead up, Norman, for pity's sake!'

I looked to my right and there was John, standing in the sea 10 yards away.

'That's just what I'm trying to do, but that Bass ain't doing much to help!' I yelled back.

'That's one hell of a fish,' was his reply.

Whether or not John did it in his enthusiasm or as a matter of help I will never probably know, but he suddenly began to run and wade out towards the scar.

'Keep back!' I screamed at him, my eyes following the thin line of light that was my line, which was getting nearer, ever nearer to the razor edges of that scar. The Spindrift was now in almost a perfect semicircle, held as far away to my left as my arms would reach, the line almost singing in its tension. I dare not give more and it seemed in that black minute that all was lost. It was not though, for John, unheeding my scream, had waded on and had reached the scar. Then the strain eased, and I realised that the fish had turned, and was now making yet another run for the open sea. But now it was tired, and its charges were much easier, shorter, and I knew it was now my turn to dictate terms. I had now backed up as far as the shallows, and the Bass was in sight, lying on its side in the shallowing water as the runs of surf returned to the sea. A Bass; a fish of size, the long soft green back, flashing silvery flanks and a belly of stark white, a big Bass that made all the griefs of yesterday become insignificant. I ran to it, and in a returning small wave pulled it the last few yards to the utter safety of the dry beach, I fell onto the fish and heaved it up into my arms with a shriek of pure delight.

'You lucky bastard,' said John, his face a mass of smiles. 'That'll be a close un to the magic weight.' (10 lb.)

I walked slowly back across the beach towards the gear, wondering if it was John's action in walking towards the scar that had turned the Bass's head. As I reached the rock shelves that housed our gear, I gently laid the Bass down on the sand, and looked at her. She was a magnificent fish, by far the best Bass I had ever had, and certainly not far off 10 lb. I lifted her head up gently, and saw the hook firmly embedded in the corner of the mouth. I removed the hook with

Just over 9 lbs . . . The author's bass caught at Noel Strand, Co Kerry

long-nosed pliers and saw that the deep amber eyes of the fish were watching me with what appeared to be a degree of interest. I weighed her with great care: 9½ lb exactly.

I took some photos, and then easing her carefully up into my arms I walked back across the beach, waded out and held her by the stock of the tail for quite some time. With each wave that went through, you could feel her strength return, until at last she shuddered against my hand and was gone.

I had not kept an eye on John or Fred in all this time, and when I looked across I saw that they were both into fish. I ran towards John just as he was drawing onto the beach yet another bar of pure silver.

'Hell's bells!' I said. 'It must be alive with Bass out there!'

'And for once we are here to take advantage of the fact,' said John, taking the offered scales from my outstretched hand.

'Well,' I asked, 'what does she go to?'

'Just over nine pounds.'

I ran back to my rod as though I had wings on my feet.

We fished on, and continued to take Bass. We did not have very many, but what we did have were of superb quality. I had another fish of 7½ lb about an hour after my first, and John had two fish of 7 lb and one of 6½ lb; while Fred, far over the left of us, had one of 8 lb, two of 5 lb, and one of 4 lb on the last worm we had between us.

We drove back in silence, and we did not bother to unpack the car when we arrived at the white-walled hotel. In one accord we all walked straight into the brightly lit bar.

'Cora!' said Fred, 'Thar can open up yon champers and clag it in three pints of that Irish Cream.'

'Gentlemen,' replied Cora, looking into our smiling faces, 'it will be a pleasure.'

So, having found Noel Strand, what follows is a record of Bass catches on this lovely beach:

<u>Monday 19th October</u>
Noel Strand: grey overcast. No wind.
A narrow beach set between headlands with stream running into bay.
Modest surf. High water on arrival.
Fred: two Bass (one of 4 lb and one of 2½ lb).
Ian: four Bass (one of 9 lb, two fish each exactly 7 lb, and one fish of 6½ lb).
Nav: two Bass (one of 9½ lb and one of 7½ lb).

<u>Tuesday, 20th October</u>
Noel Strand: grey overcast, rain, much cooler than Monday, fished ebb.
John: two Bass (one of 6¼ lb and a 'schoolie').
We caught 112¼ lb of Bass, most of them of quality. Every fish caught was safely returned to the water.

In my fishing diary of 1970 I wrote: 'My Bass had a profound affect upon my angling and I had no inclination to go fishing at all upon my return to the UK.' As the months passed, I found my love of angling grew back from its period of satisfied leisure to its old state of keen anticipation.

I did return to Waterville in early September 1971, on honeymoon. I did go fishing; I fished Reenroe at the top of the tide on the Wednesday morning of our second week. I took a Bass of over 8 lb, on a Bruce & Walker Spindrift with an Abu 6500, ledgering a single lugworm. The Bass was in absolutely mint condition and was returned safely after being photographed.

Put like that it seems a non-event, yet the Bass weighed over 8 lb and was a cracker that went extremely well on my light tackle. That I took my life in my hands to put my bait as far out as I could is not mentioned, but it should be. I did take a calculated risk, something that one should only do on occasion and after a lot of thought. On this occasion this decision was taken without a second thought, which was stupid, to say the least of it. In mitigation the sight of the feeding

The author's honeymoon bass that went just over 8 lbs!

gannets beyond the breaking surf line had been the decision-maker for me and as I had waded out prior to casting, the sea had fallen away substantially so the decion could be said as having being made for me.

By now the water was about knee-deep, the sea had fallen away, it was almost flat calm. So I decided to wade further out (I had chest-high waders on) and went on as far as I dared. The moment the cast was made, the lead flying up and outwards from me, the surf came back with a vengeance. As I turned to get back into shallower water, my rod and reel held close to my chest the first breaking wave hit me and went directly over me. How I kept my balance I do not know, but I did somehow. Then after staggering a few more yards towards the beach I was hit again by the following wave, but this had little effect save to add to a very wet head of hair.

On arrival on the beach I had probably a dozen turns of line left on the reel spool, no more, and so the bait was at least 140 yards or more from the beach and very close to the beginning of the breaking surf line. Now the story has some body and truth to it, worthy of a very memorable fish.

There is one further matter I must include here, and that is the question of secrecy. In our current society, fishing reports as published in the angling press are read avidly by members of the fishing industry, and invariably acted upon. This question of secrecy is a sensitive matter that involves every angler, whatever his personal fishing discipline. If you find a fishing spot that produces fish every time you go to fish it, do you tell? Your fishing mates? Probably. Anyone else? For me, 'No!' As well as the Noel Strand affair, I inadvertently told a trusted sea angler friend, over a pint in Dingle, that we had had a good week's fishing at Derrynane. Not thinking anything unusual about his questions and believing him a friend of integrity, I told him essentially what we had caught. The following morning, just after dawn, a Dingle-based keelboat made its way into Derrynane Bay and trawled it. This was witnessed by two visiting UK anglers who had camped by the beach so as to fish it at high water that very morning. They fished the tide down and had not a touch despite excellent conditions, and could only put their lack of success down to the illegal actions of that keelboat. Furthermore, there were no reports of any Bass being taken from this beach for some time afterwards. I discovered later that my 'friend' worked for a fish processor in Dingle.

Secrecy came up again when I wrote 'A Touch of Irish Cream'. I was asked by the then editor of the magazine *Angling* exactly where was the stretch of beach that featured in the story. Being Brian Harris, who I had then known for ten years, I told him but added the caveat that if he could would he please keep the location as secret as possible. He agreed, and for the next six years the secret was kept. Every now and then I'd read an article in *Angling* and it was obvious to me at least that the writer had been let in on the secret; but since these writers were usually the leading lights of the day and never was the location given, I was very happy.

However, secrets nowadays are all but impossible to keep, and this was no exception; that it had held for as long as it did was exceptional. The March 1977 issue of the *Sea Angler* broke it to the world, with the front cover of the magazine showing Des Brennan, the famous IFT representative, holding up a fine *dead* Bass with three more good Bass, *likewise dead*, whilst behind him was Noel Strand in all its glory! In the article that accompanied the pictorial spread the author Mr Peter Collins actually wrote, 'Let me tell you of my paradise, confident that you will enjoy it as much as I did. I even suspect that perhaps a dozen of the 36,000 readers of this magazine know it already and will heave deep sighs and call for the blood of Collins when I name it.'

My blood boiled. Had I ever met Mr Collins at that time I do not know what I would have done or said to him. Collins admitted in the same article that it was Des Brennan who had taken him there, and since it was Brennan's job to publicise as much as he was able the wonders of Irish rod and line fishing, the reason he did it is obvious.

How did Brennan get to know? Almost certainly one of the secret-holders told him of it, and maybe even took him there. Anyway, the secret was out now. I wonder how many days after publication the first of the Dingle trawlers swept into the bay flanking the strand we called Noel, that had given us so much pleasure. It did not take long, I bet!

Sometime in the late eighties I heard a story of what happened to two friends of mine during their annual holiday in County Kerry after the Bass. It was an unusual story as I have heard, and...

Amalgam

It was dark. The sea slight against the steeply banked beach, high water now past, a good hour to moonrise, and a line of fishing rods, their tips lit by the headlights of the anglers and the glare of the odd Tilley lamp set tight against the cliff foot behind them. My rod standing on its rest was on the outside of the line, bent slightly to the pull of the tide, unmoving as it had been for most of the day. I was just beginning to feel the cold of the night, and as I stamped my feet two figures came over towards me and stood silent for a moment.

'Hey up, what's thee after?' I asked.

'Nowt. Just bored witless that's all,' answered the closest of the two.

'Aye, its a bit grim I must admit. Not a touch all flamin' day!'

'Tell me,' answered Ron. 'What's it like, then, Ireland? I've heard its over-rated. Like, not as good as its painted.'

'Don't you believe it, it's one 'ell of a place, believe me. A darn sight better than over here, as sure as 'ell better than this defunct pond here!' With this contemptuous remark the second of the two figures, Fred, aimed a kick at an imaginary ball and wandered off into the dark.

'Look, Ron,' I said, 'Fred's right, not that you need telling just how bad it is over 'ere. Dammit all, think on, tonight: a good tide, a good sea, a bucket of great bait, just cold enough, and all for nowt. Its perfect really, couldn't wish for it better, but ner a bite, not even a bloody line bite. A few years ago ...'

'I know, Norman, we'd have had a sack full afore now. Nay thou don't have to convince me how bad things are. But Ireland? Well, you hear so much abou it, ah'm just getting to disbelieve everything about these great fishing spots, that's all.'

'Go on, Norman, tell 'im aboot Bouncer and 'is mate Horace!' called Fred from out of the night, 'Yer know the one ah mean.'

'Strewth, Norman, not another of your flamin' yarns. Who for the love of a good woman is Bouncer? Angler is he? From around 'ere? Ah've never 'eard on 'im.'

'Bouncer is a bloke we know, he fishes around here sometimes. Horace is 'is mate, almost inseparable they are, both fishing mad.'

'Bouncer is a huge fellah. Well, he's over six foot and big wi' it. Don't suffer fools gladly, believe me. Don't get me wrong, he's easy-going and like all big fellahs he's gentle with it, but when it comes to fishing, well, they are both very single-minded gentlemen, and that's the truth. Bouncer has his own small boat an' all, gets off frey Filey, Bridlington and sometimes gets off 'ere too. You've probably seen him yourself and, well, Bouncer is our name for 'im, that's all. The pair of em go all over t' place, as fancy takes 'em: Cornwall, Dunge, Suffolk coast or up ti Scotland, but they both love Ireland and go there as often as they can. Anyway, I christened him Bouncer and the name stuck and us lot allus refer to 'im as that.'

Ron broke open a new packet of cigarettes and offered me one, took one for himself and lit us both up. The pause in the story had given me time to reflect and remember the story that Fred had referred to.

'C'mon, Norman, ger on wi' it. There's nowt worse than waitin'!' said Fred, who had now returned from the dark.

Bouncer and Horace always used to go to County Kerry in late September, and always to the same place. They stayed in the same hotel and after a couple of visits had got that part of Kerry, near Fenit, well lined up as far as the fishing went, and that was especially true of the Bass fishing. They found a beach that had a stream running onto it, a good run of Bass and more to the point it was always deserted, having no bathers, surfers, kids or other anglers.

They even began to look on this beach as very much their own and after all the time and effort they put into fishing it they could be forgiven for that. That September, the beach lived up to its reputation, with a number of good Bass taken, and every day since they arrived they found the beach deserted, and this despite the fact that at that time of year more and more anglers were going to Ireland after the Bass, especially Kerry, so that lonely, deserted beaches tended to be harder to find.

However, on this particular morning they arrived to find a large estate car complete with a bright yellow caravan parked on the narrow grass strip that flanked both the stream and the access road that gave the entry to the beach. It was early and the thin grey light of dawn had only just begun to pierce the gloom of the night that still showed stars against the blue black of the western sky.

'Wonder who it is? Some anglers yer reckon?' said Horace as they began to unload their car.

'Could be,' replied Bouncer. 'But if it were there'd be signs of life by now. Looks like who ever it is is still asleep.'

'On a morning like this, wi' a sea like that running!' Horace raised his arm as he spoke, and pointed to the long line of white breaking surf that was showing more clearly now as the morning light continued to improve.

'Can't be anglers and sleep through that racket, that's for sure,' said Bouncer.

'Aye, and they could be deaf,' said Horace diffidently.

'They'd bloody well 'ave to be. Now come on and let's get going; it'll be full light soon and we'll have missed the best time.'

Conditions that morning were ideal. There was no wind, the surf was regular and high, producing wide flat tables of water that were beginning to reach well up the beach as the tide made. They had decided that they would fish about 10 yards beyond the entry point of the stream into the sea, and move back closer to the stream as the tide came onto high water.

They fished hard, taking half a dozen Bass between them, the best going to a good 6 lb, but they missed more than they landed, including one that had Bouncer almost at his wits end. The bite was almost imperceptible, almost a brush upon the line; Bouncer's reaction had been instinctive. He swept the rod back over his left shoulder until the rod stopped dead in its arc, and was jerked back down so hard that he almost fell over. Regaining his balance as best he could, holding the rod upright and keeping the line as tight as he dare, he began to retrieve the line. Slowly the line was recovered and the fish brought ever closer to the tideline, the surf regular and even, not causing too much difficulty until a heavy back run of water from an unusually heavy run of surf hit an incoming wave with Bouncer's Bass in the midst of it. He had not been quick enough in easing the pressure on rod or line, but suddenly aware that the pressure he was inadvertently applying to both the line and rod was too much he eased off the drag and the thus the line, which now went slack. The Bass with the heavier press of water upon its flank, and in one desperate effort to regain its freedom, used the full weight of the fast-retreating wave and violently shook its head. The hook trace broke, Bouncer's rod bounced back, the weight gone, and for a moment in the lifting, turning wave Bouncer saw the long, light green back, the deep flanks, the broad heavy tail. Bouncer stood at the tide's edge and wondered as he swore and swore at his luck and misfortune of it.

'What d'yer reckon it'd gone?' asked Horace to a still sullen and unusually morose Bouncer a little later. They had broken off to eat, and drink coffee from their flasks.

'Dunno. Wor a good un though, best I've ever had on 'ere or anywhere. I saw it for a moment … that's summat, I suppose. It's still got me 'ook in it, an' all. Worr a good un.'

'Yeah, it looked good from where I was. Put a lovely ol' 'eave hoo in yer rod, it did. Must have been well over ten pounds that one, don't yer think?'

Bouncer did not answer. He was still reliving those nerve-tingling minutes and wondering if in fact it had been his fault that he had lost it.

'C'mon, what d'yer reckon? You must have a good idea,' said Horace prodding gently.

'Well, aye … ah reckon it wor more than any ten pounds, a deal more. And the power of it, strewth, Horace! Its best not talked about, not now anyway.'

'Yeah, I can understand that.' said Horace slapping his friend on his slumped shoulders.

The day progressed, the sun was high now, pouring from a clear blue sky, and with the passing of high water the Bass had seemingly gone too. Bouncer, with that instinctive feeling for knowing that the Bass had gone, called a halt, saying to Horace that he'd lost the feeling for it and if anything fancied a Guinness. Horace, knowing his friend well, acceded to the suggestion and so they began to organise themselves for their trip back to their car. It was then that they saw him; or rather the two of them. They were making their way through the dunes down to the side of the stream, walking with a resolute purpose directly towards Horace and Bouncer.

The man was of slight build, wearing a vivid multicoloured shirt, the sleeves rolled up to the elbows. The long-legged khaki shorts revealed a pair of knobbly knees, the shorts suspended with a pair of equally garish braces that contrasted violently with the shirt. Upon his head was a straw Panama hat with a broad ribbon that matched the shirt in colour. His companion was a good foot taller and reminded Horace immediately of Edith Sitwell on a good day. She wore what could only be described as a sarong, its colour and pattern identical to the man's shirt, but it had little shape, revealing bony shoulders and long, very skinny legs, scarred with the lumps and bumps of varicose veins. They walked directly up to where Bouncer and Horace were standing as they prepared themselves for their walk back to the car.

'Oh, you're anglers, then?' said the woman.

Horace, resisting the urge to respond in an equally naive way, replied meekly that they were. His views on seeing them on his beloved beach could not really be properly expressed; it was not friendly at all.

'We are very keen to go fishing,' she said utterly unaware of the animosity that was poorly hidden in the hearts and minds of both

Horace and Bouncer. 'We've heard and read so much about it, and since we are here in Ireland, we feel we should have a go, and catch something for breakfast!'

The disbelief that spread across Bouncer's face had to be seen to be believed. 'Have you fished before?' Bouncer asked.

'Oh, no, no, never been fishing before, either of us,' she replied.

'Fresh water?' asked Horace.

'No, never been fishing at all. You see we've been …', she paused and looked towards her companion as though looking for a prompt, but he remained silent, '… fortunate, quite lucky really … something that happened to us. And so we bought … you must have seen it when you arrived this morning?'

'The caravan?' said Bouncer.

'Yes, the caravan. Yes, well, we bought that and the car that goes with it, and we've come on a grand tour. We've been on tour all summer but it is only now that we've wanted to go fishing.'

Bouncer and Horace looked at each other and suppressed the feelings that each knew the other had, that these idiots were going to pollute their beautiful and much-loved beach with their presence.

'How do you start?' asked the little man. 'I mean, what do you do? Where do you go? Where did you get your … tackle from?' He looked at the rods lying across the rucksacks and the buckets.

'Well,' said Bouncer, 'we bought them in England, built them ourselves. They are a special kind of rod you see, designed for a special type of fishing.'

'Oh, is there anywhere around here I could buy … tackle?'

Bouncer thought about Tralee and wondered if there was a tackle shop there and concluded that there must be, of sorts, but whether it would have what he would want them to have or what they should have, was another matter altogether.

'Probably in Tralee,' he replied. 'Yeah, you'd better try Tralee, or failing that you might have to go to Limerick, or failing that, Cork. There'll certainly be something in Limerick or Cork.'

'You could try Killarney too,' said Horace.

'Aye, Killarney. I'd forgotten about Killarney,' added Bouncer.

'But what should we buy?'

'How long 'ave you got, a year? Five years?' muttered Horace under his breath.

But Bouncer, trying to be a little bit courteous, continued getting his gear together and looking at the little man said, 'And how much money are you prepared to spend?'

'Oh, money does not come into it at all, there's no question about how much it's going to cost. We want the best you see, really good stuff.'

'Steady, steady now, Ernest, you don't want to waste your money. You know, you might not even like it!'

'Yes, well, that's true I suppose. But I still want to go fishing, Hilda, let's put it that way.'

'Well, you need a rod, you need a reel like this one. This one is Swedish, that won't be difficult to remember, you can see what it looks like. That's it, really.'

'Bouncer,' interrupted Horace, 'don't you think he should really have a mangle? I mean a fixed spool reel, him being a novice, like?'

So Bouncer explained the difference between the reels and talked about their rods and went into all the deep intracacies of fishing, as his thirst for his lunchtime Guinness continued to get even stronger. Eventually, he reached the point that Horace knew from the start was going to come.

'And where d'yer get yer bait? And what kind of bait?' He then bent down as he said it and removed the lid from the top of the plastic bucket.

'Ugh!' cried out Hilda. 'What are those horrible things?'

'Those are worms, dear,' said Horace, quickly replacing the lid on the bucket.

'Sand worms,' said Bouncer. 'Like earthworms except they live in the sand and not in soil.'

'And how do yer get those?' asked Ernest.

'With great difficulty,' said Horace. 'Well, you have to dig for them, its quite an art.'

'But where do you dig them?'

Horace bristled. Under his breath, as controlled as he could whisper it, he muttered darkly, 'Don't tell 'em, don't tell 'em!' For beaches that held good bait were very few and far between. They existed alright but you did not go around telling anyone where they were.

'See the tackle dealer. Talk to 'im, he'll help yer,' said Horace, trying to close the way this conversation was going.

'You could use Mackerel,' continued Bouncer, as if Horace had not spoken at all. 'You know, you can buy it in Tralee, cut it into strips …'

'Now look 'ere,' said Horace, becoming ever more frustrated, 'we've got to be off now, we're late as it is. But we may see you again … Are you going off on your travels again soon?'

'Oh no,' said Hilda, 'we think this is a beautiful place, the nicest place we've seen so far on our travels, so quiet and so secluded.'

'Tell us about it,' thought Bouncer to himself, giving Horace a quick look.

'And the sound of the sea is so sleep-conducive, its lovely. Oh no, we'll be here for a few more days at least, maybe a week more.' She looked wistfully at her husband whose attention was on the rods and their rings.

'Bang goes our holiday!' thought Horace. 'Bloody visitors!'

With the prospect of having lost the absolute isolation of their fishing filling the thoughts of both of them, and unable to look at each other for fear of saying what they were thinking, certain to be overheard by Ernest or Hilda who followed close behind them, they made their way off the beach.

The days passed. Horace and Bouncer continued in their fishing but did not return to their beach. Instead they fished from Fenit Pier, and went off in the boats to fish for Tope, big Skate and Monkfish that inhabited Tralee Bay. But despite the quality of the fishing their hearts were not in it, and they both agreed that for the last few days of the stay they had to go back to the beach, even if it meant meeting up with Hilda and Ernest again, for their arrival had taken away something from the place that they both looked upon as very much their own.

'The 'ell wi' it,' said Horace. 'Let's go back tomorrow, its high water just after five p.m. The forecast ain't good, promising gale force winds, and with our beach being so exposed ah don't think it'll be fishable come Saturday, and by then, well, we'll be on our way 'ome.'

'Alright,' said Bouncer, 'tomorrow it is. We dig some bait tonight, get there for low water and fish tide up!'

'Done!' replied Horace.

The next day after a leisurely lie-in they set off, each thinking that this was certainly the last time they would come down the long lane to the beach on this holiday. The caravan and the estate car were still parked as they had been that other morning, but of the occupants there was no sign.

They unpacked quietly and quickly got themselves down through the dunes past the edge of the stream and onto the beach. The beach, now fully exposed at low water, revealed Ernest and Hilda fishing side by side in the exact spot where Horace and Bouncer had intended to fish.

'That's torn it!' said Horace. 'What are we going to do now?'

'Oh, come on,' replied Bouncer, 'it don't matter if we fish this side of t'stream or t'other. They just happen to have the spot that we like.'

'Not wi' owt bloody good reason!' countered Horace. 'Tide moves along there, an' you pick up whatever fish are comin' t' stream on that side, not on this. Dammit, Bouncer, we've proved it often enough in t' past, they just don't move on this beach the other way.'

Bouncer ignored him and made his way along the flat beach down towards the sea's edge, Horace reluctantly coming along behind. They began to tackle up, preparing themselves for the coming session, Horace mumbling continually under his breath, Bouncer ignoring him as best he could.

They'd been there for no more than five minutes and Bouncer had started to make his way to the sea's edge when suddenly he heard a shout, and looked towards Horace, thinking it was he who had shouted. But it was Hilda, who was running along the beach towards them, dressed as before except this time her sarong was augmented with a half-buttoned cardigan. Her face was wreathed in smiles.

'Hello! Hello!' she cried. 'We've caught some fish! Flatfish. And we've had bites, quite violent, sometimes very gentle ones that ... well we don't know what they were, but the rods went, you know. But we didn't feel anything when we picked the rods up.'

'You got you sens sorted, then?' asked Horace feigning interest he did not feel. 'Got some bait an' all? Did ya?'

'Well, we bought some Mackerel as you had said, and that seems to do alright. We've had a lovely breakfast of flatfish this morning!' said Hilda smiling all over her face.

'Very good,' said Horace wondering what it was they had had for breakfast and how they'd gone about preparing the fish.

'OK, then love, well done. You can tell us later, but you'd better go now, we too want a good day today.'

'Yes, surely,' said Hilda who then turned around and went back, splashing through the stream.

'Would you bloody credit it!' said Horace. 'They've actually caught summat. Amazin'!'

'Nay, don't be like that,' said Bouncer quite lamely. 'They've got a right to fish, I suppose. It's just that we look on this spot as our own, and it isn't right, Horace.' He turned back to continue his walk into the surf, impatient to get fishing.

'The 'ell wi' that!' yelled back Horace. 'It is ours, we've fished it long enough to own the bloody freehold!'

Bouncer looked back at his friend and smiled at the concept of beach ownership.

They fished on through the afternoon till the early evening, taking nothing for their troubles or efforts. Both Bouncer and Horace kept looking along the beach towards Ernest and Hilda, but they had taken nothing either. Eventually high tide came and went, the ebb set in. The best time, they thought, had now passed and Bouncer reluctantly said they'd best be off, they'd much to do before they left the next morning. Slowly they packed up, waved their goodbyes to Ernest and Hilda, and made their way up to where the stream left the dunes and the path that led back to their car.

No sooner had they begun to walk through the dunes to the car than they heard shouts and screams behind them. They stopped and looked back towards the beach. Hilda was jumping up and down, screaming at the top of her voice for them to come back. Seeing that both Bouncer and Horace were in fact coming back to the beach, she set off running back the way she'd come, towards her husband. As Bouncer and Horace got onto the beach they looked towards Ernest who was standing knee-deep in the surf, both hands grasping the butt of a tight-curved glass rod whose whiteness stood stark against the dark, brooding backcloth of the distant hills.

'Bloody 'ell!' yelled out Horace 'I don't believe it, look at that rod, you could lift the *Titanic* wi' that bloody thing, look at the bend onnit!'

'Must 'ave a Tope!' said Bouncer. 'He's using Mackerelstrip after all. It won't last long wi' a nylon hook trace, that's for sure! But c'mon, Horace, let's show willing and give 'im an 'and!'

They ran across the still wet beach to where Hilda stood, her arms clasped around her body.

'It almost pulled the rod out of its stand, it did!' she said.

Ernest, a resolute look upon his face, the straw Panama tight across the top of his eyes, was winding hard, the rod going over and over into an increasingly tighter curve.

'No! No! No! Be gentle, for pity's sakes!' yelled Bouncer. 'Don't be too hard on the rod, the fish, give it some line when it wants it. Don't let it go against the waves in this ebb or you'll lose it!'

Ernest suddenly released the pressure on the rod and began to backwind. The strain upon the curved rod eased considerably. Horace looked seawards, his eyes following the line as it glinted in the last of the evening's sunlight. There in the water was the biggest Bass that Horace had ever seen. It was huge.

Bouncer yelled at Horace, 'The gaff! Horace, go get the gaff!'

'We didn't bring it,' said Horace.

'Oh, bloody 'ell!' said Bouncer. 'Ernest, back up the beach. Ernest, d'yer 'ear me? Back up the beach, but slowly, slowly.'

Ernest, hearing Bouncer's cries, began to walk backwards up the beach, one hand firm on the reel, the other firmly grasping the butt of the rod. As they watched, the Bass came through the falling-away surf, all fight now gone, just laid upon its side, exhausted, totally beaten. As it slid the last few feet the sea fell completely away, exposing the full size of the fish. It was huge, to the absolutely disbelieving eyes of Horace and Bouncer.

'Gee wilikers!' said Horace. 'Its ginormous! Enormous! I didn't believe that Bass like that existed any more, and on our beach an' all!'

'It could 'ave been ours,' said Bouncer quietly, almost to himself, 'if we'd been 'ere first to fish it.'

'Yeah, yeah,' whispered Horace, not really hearing fully the words of Bouncer, but instinctively knowing what it was that he had said.

Bouncer ran forward and slid his left hand under the belly of the Bass, grasped the stock of the tail with his right hand and lifted the fish tight up against his chest, turned, and ran back up the beach towards Ernest, who was standing stock still and open-mouthed.

'Is it a good one?' asked Hilda. 'It certainly put a curve into his rod, did you see that?'

'Yes,' said Horace, 'its a wonderful fish, a fantastic fish, the biggest Bass I've ever seen. Didn't think Bass like that were even … made.'

Bouncer laid the Bass down upon the sand. It was indeed huge, soft-green-backed, silver-white-flanked, white-bellied with a heavy broad tail, tight head. The hook, with its heavy nylon trace, firmly bedded in the hard gristle of the upper jaw took some removal, but at last Bouncer had it out.

'Hey!' said Horace. 'What's that there, on t'other side?'

'What?' asked Bouncer.

'Look! You've taken my hook out but there's still summat hanging from its mouth. What is it? Another hook? Is it?'

'Yes, there's still …' Bouncer carefully lifted up the Bass's head and gently eased open the mouth. There, tight in the corner of the mouth, was a short length of nylon and buried deep in the bend of the lower jaw, partly hidden, was a fine wire hook of very recent vintage.

'Oh yes,' said Bouncer, 'it's another hook alright. And a broken trace. Somebody else must have had this on, and not too long ago, looking at the state of that hook. Some unlucky angler.'

'Its a big fish, and we want it for tea!' said Hilda.

'Ye gods!' Horace cried out. 'You're not going to kill it, lass? You'll not do that? Kill a Bass? That Bass?'

'Whyever not? It's just another fish, isn't it? It'll do nicely and there's enough of it to do several days teas for both of us.'

'I 'ope it bloody well chokes you both!'

'Alright,' said Bouncer, 'she's your fish, you caught it, you do what you want with it.'

And Bouncer laid the Bass back down on the beach. He stood up. Looking down upon the fish with full eyes he took his priest from the pouch that hung from his belt and quickly dispatched the Bass, that lifted and flapped its tail hard upon the sand as the blow was struck. Horace sighed deeply and turned his face away from an act that to him was both wicked and obscene.

'We'll be off now,' said Bouncer. 'We'll not be back. We're off 'ome tomorrow and by the look of that sky and this freshening wind ...' he pointed off to the south-west where the last vestiges of light showed a blue-black cloud that towered to the limits of their vision, 'you'll not be fishing here tomorrow.'

'Oh, we're going to move on too now, we are leaving in the morning, going north up into Clare or on to Donegal. We've enjoyed the fishing so much here that we'll try to do some more up there,' said Ernest.

'You should take that fish,' said Bouncer, pointing to the Bass, 'into Tralee and get it weighed. Don't gut it, whatever you do. Take it to the shop where you got your tackle. But you must get it weighed.'

'What d'yer reckon it goes, Bouncer?' asked Horace.

'Dunno, fifteen pounds at the least, probably a deal more. There's a set of scales back there in my gear, they're not spot on, but they'll give us a good idea.

They did weigh the Bass outside the door to the caravan. It was too dark to see the marker of the scales clearly, but the Bass went over the 17 lb point.

Bouncer and Horace left for home the next morning and had been home for four weeks when they saw a report in the angling press that said a local record Bass of 17½ lb had been caught in Kerry, by an angler from Wiltshire who was on a touring holiday in Ireland.

'It was a marvellous fish for the area,' said a spokesman for where the fish had been weighed.

Soon it was forgotten, the autumn came and went and the winter was fast upon them when they saw a further report in the angling press. The Bass had won a holiday for the captor and his wife, all expenses paid.

'Did you read it?' asked Horace as he and Bouncer had a pint in their local pub.

'Aye,' replied Bouncer. 'I did.'

'They'd won t' Pools, yer know. A fair old sum by all accounts.'

'How d'yer know?' asked Bouncer.

'Nora, barmaid at our 'otel, told me that last Friday night. She'd heard this woman talking in the butcher's during that week and it turned out it were 'Ilda.'

'Why didn't yer tell me?'

'It were a sensitive subject that Bass, and you've never said a word about it from that day to this.'

'There were no need.'

'I saw the hook you know. Ah made a point of lookin' after we'd weighed it. It were your 'ook and no mistake. Can't give you it, mind, but if you push me hard, like, I'd 'ave to say it were your fish. I mean, he couldn't 'ave failed to land it wi' that 'awser he were using, could he?'

It was suddenly cold and I wanted to be off. After all, the Board was not more than ten minutes away. Telling the story of Bouncer and the Bass had brought it all back, even to remembering the pained look Bouncer had given me when Horace had told the story the previous summer.

'True that, eh Norman?' asked Ron.

'So I was told, aye, it's true. Typical of fishing that, innit: them than can, can't and them that can't, can catch all the bleedin' great fish that swim!'

'And don't look at me in that tone of voice when you say that!' said Fred out of the darkness to our right.

I last visited Ireland in 1976 and have missed my holidays there immensely. All I ever found in Ireland (save the Belfast episode, and there were good reasons for that) was kindness, a generosity of spirit I have found nowhere else – an altogether lovely place, Ireland, and I recommend any reader of this book who fancies a trip there not to hesitate for a moment but GO! And enjoy it all as we certainly did.

Thereafter, 1963–1976

In January of 1963 I saw an advert for a post as a junior quantity surveyor, to work in Scarborough. Apart from being amazed at the location of the job within 8 miles of my home, I saw that it offered a reasonable salary. I applied.

I started work in Scarborough at the beginning of May 1963 and a whole new life opened before me; for one thing, pretty much above everything else I very much wanted to get back into sea fishing, and that meant starting from scratch. As if in pursuit of this ambition, three things of importance happened that summer: one of seeming little consequence at the the time but was to have a lasting appeal; the second was to bring to fruition a keen interest in boats; the third was to observe two anglers having a casting competition.

The innocuous event was just that. One lunch time in late June of 1963, I went to find some lunch, then I decided to buy a newspaper. I made my way to Scarborough Railway Station to buy a newspaper and I found on W.H. Smith's magazine and newspaper display stand a new fishing magazine called *Creel*. Its affect upon me was to be profound and together with *Angling* magazine that succeeded *Creel* five years later, continued to have a serious effect upon both my fishing interests and by inference my life.

The second event of importance was *Cameron Rose*.

Good Day

We bought *Cameron Rose* in December 1963, a sturdy, clinker-built motorboat, typical of the type of boat one sees taking visitors for trips. Between April and mid-June, every available weekend, and evenings when possible, were spent working on the boat. With professional advice we completely re-ribbed her (a difficult task for those who have never done anything like it before), and two new cross-timbers were inserted. By late June all was finished, the boat sparkled in her new paint, and to see her laid on her wheels ready for her first fishing trip was worth all the blisters, cuts and pulled muscles we had suffered over the previous three months. We felt justly proud, and very excited.

During the weeks of work we would occasionally break off to talk over the hoped-for good summer. Prolonged periods of warm settled weather were wanted, and if that came, with it would come Mackerel. Mackerel! The name suggests humid days, deeply curving rods, excitement and thrills. Up on the Yorkshire coast, Mackerel are welcomed by everyone who owns a light rod. Mackerel would renew our faith in fishing. The past winter and others before it had brought little success in return for the hours of patient angling on cold, windswept scars and cliffs. Mackerel, that great sporting little fish, offers a fight on light tackle second to none, and is, we think, pound for pound, the strongest fish in the sea. Their arrival is always welcomed with wide smiles and the great anticipation of thrills to come.

So it was June 1964. We were all tingling with anticipation that Tuesday night since we had heard that the longliners out of

103

Scarborough had been among shoals of Mackerel. With our light glass-fibre rods and small reels, we pushed *Cameron Rose* from her berth, along the landing, and down to the sea. The tide was ebbing and we wanted to be at our predetermined spot for slack water and the first of the flood. We got her afloat, the wheels were pulled off and taken by Joe beyond the high-water mark. As we waited for Joe to return, we looked towards the Brigg, where we could see great hordes of diving and wheeling birds. What excitement that aroused, for those birds were the sign of the britt and the hoped-for Mackerel. 'Hurry up, Joe,' we all thought as he trudged back down the beach, and sensing our haste he ran through the shallows to the boat. The engine fired first time and we were off to an evening's fishing that none of us would ever forget.

The sea in the bay was slightly ruffled by a south-westerly wind and the sky to the east was clear and deep blue. Behind us, dark strato-cumulus clouds were massing on the edge of the Wolds, beginning to block the sun's rays. On, out across the bay, past Pulpit and the old Roman pier, and Crab Hole, round and through the slacking tideway, and round again to the lee side of the famous Filey Brigg. Here the sea was like a lake, dark and flat, a movement so slight that it could hardly be noticed. Everywhere around us birds were feeding, diving and screaming, the water boiling with the splashes of the falling birds and leaping britt. As the boat gave way and came to anchor under High Brigg it started to rain, lightly at first, but harder as the heavy clouds cut out the face of the evening sun. It was to continue like this for the rest of the evening, and though we then cursed it as we slipped into our oilskins, within a few minutes we were not to notice our increasing dampness.

The four of us tackled up. Using 3oz leads, heavy enough to give adequate depth, yet light enough to have minimum effect on our tackle, and with three feathered hooks to the trace, we began to jig. This is to imitate the action of the britt (so-called 'sile' in the north).

Joe was first down, his lead leaving that bubbly phosphorescence in the dark green depths, and he was the first to strike. 'I'm into something, lads, what a start! This promises good.'

His rod curved deeply, the reel whined, and the excitement to join in the fun made us all fingers and thumbs. Quickly he gained control, and soon three Horse Mackerel were flapping in the fish box. Dave was next, his small rod dipped and the line cut through the opaque water; soon three more Horse Mackerel came into the boat. Tally, then myself, hit them too, as well as the occasional Coalfish. What a promising start, surely Mackerel must be here somewhere.

We had no sooner thought it than my rod suddenly bucked as though a great hand had grabbed the line, and the reel screamed. The line slackened; I reeled furiously. I knew I had hit Mackerel, for only Mackerel can take like that – a hard, solid strike – and then the run to the top. Yes! There they were, 20 yards from the boat, diving, running, splashing.

Oh, the excitement, our first Mackerel of the season, and on our first sea trip. Soon the cry was up – 'We're among 'em!' – and with rods dipping and lines running everywhere it was not surprising when they began to cross, and anguished cries of excited anglers rent the sodden air. No thought was given to the unrelenting rain. All around me I could hear, 'Ay ay, here we go again', as yet another rod dipped and a reel screamed. Every now and again, though, the rod would thump heavily, the tip would dip into the water, the rod shaking like the devil had possession of it, and for a few minutes you would hold hard, unable to do anything except exert as much pressure as you dared on the light tackle, and pump the fish slowly, gently to the surface.

These were no Mackerel, but Codling, and good ones, their heads shaking vigorously as they surged downwards in an effort to get to the kelp jungle below. Codling of 3 to 5 lb, in peak condition. Mackerel in mid-water and Cod below them, this was what we'd hoped for, but never thought would happen, especially on our first trip. This was fishing plus.

It was just after the Codling had been boated that Joe had a great take. No mistaking that solid, boring weight: Pollack. Pollack, hanging in the lee of the submerged reefs waiting for the Sand Eels to come down on the tide, had fallen for the feathers. Three pollack came to the gaff within the next 20 minutes or so. Pollack, so rare of late, where once there were myriads of them, off the sunken reefs of Filey Brigg.

The fishing had been so marvellous that night was fast upon us and we had to cease. Up came the anchor and the engine fired first time, around came her head and we were going home. With Tally at the tiller we looked at the result of our 90 minutes' fishing – Coalfish, Horse Mackerel, Mackerel, Codling and Pollack – a grand total of 14 stone of fish.

We leaned back and sat for the first time. The rain had ceased and the wind was freshening from the south-east. We looked at each other and saw that look that can only be seen in anglers who've had a day to remember.

Although the partnership of *Cameron Rose* changed over the next six years the original nucleus of Tally Abbott, David Johnson (and of course his Father Bill) and myself remained throughout the partnership. Arguments, though never fierce, did become a more regular occurrence over the years, especially about replacing the Morris 8 series E engine (circa 1935!), something that should have happened but never did. Essentially because to do so would have involved all four partners in a costly liability when they had other more pressing demands on their wage packets, like wives or girlfriends. Despite all the problems, mainly minor thank goodness, it was a successful and happy boat and we had some memorable days.

One that comes readily to mind was a Sunday in July when Dave Johnson, Tally Abbott, Martin Scotter and myself found ourselves over what must have been a very large shoal of fish (Mackerel, Horse Mackerel, Coalfish and Cod), all feeding avidly on Herring sile at a spot called Rock Edge in Filey Bay. For a very short while we shared a killing spree of taking Cod between 6 and 12 lb, two at a time to all four rods. While it lasted it was pure madness! Cries for the gaff, the foulest language you can imagine as two 10-pounders took your line around your neighbour's solitary 12-pounder, all four of us involved at once … you did not dare put your rod down for a moment. Above us were the screaming gulls, diving, wheeling, skimming the water, all trying to get at the disturbed free offerings that were all around the boat.

A hundred yards from *Cameron Rose* on that sunny, windless Sunday morning a local cobble, *Triumph*, had a party of visiting rods aboard. Every one of these rods was, as we were, 'jigging', and of course every one of them took fish at the same time. The result was much like in *Cameron Rose*: utter chaos, mayhem. Fish, two or even three at a time, Mackerel as well as Cod, had taken the lines of the anglers and knitted them into one almighty ball of a tangled mess, not away from the boat side where the boatmen could have done something to resolve the problem, but directly under the boat!

So involved were we in our own wonderful problems that I never did find out just how *Triumph* solved the problem, because a few minutes after I saw all their rods dip into fish, almost as one rod, *Triumph* was off, taking both anglers and boat away from the area and off to calmer waters to try to solve their problem. How that was done I have no idea, save that a lot of time and patience would have been involved. All that fishing time lost!

We never did an accurate weigh-in of what we caught that memorable Sunday, but it was at least 30 stone, probably nearer 35 stone if truth be told. After we had our pick of the catch, the remainder was sold – for a pittance I must add – to visitors who flocked around *Cameron Rose* after we landed.

In 1969 David took *Cameron Rose* away to Whitby where he was now based, and he eventually settled down there. What happened to *Cameron Rose* I never found out. I am and always have been a romantic, and in view of the many happy hours spent either working on or fishing from *Cameron Rose*, this was a pretty ignominious end of which I am not proud.

Anyway, before I lost touch with *Cameron Rose* I struck lucky, a combination of having a boat, fishing from it and having a popular fisherman's pub as your local resulted in my meeting *Mary Joy*.

Mary Joy:
A Day in the Life of a Scarborough Keelboat

It is not often that what appears to be a simple and straightforward invitation to go to sea in a keelboat turns out to be such a memorable day that it is remembered for a lifetime. But such was the invitation that came from the skipper of the keelboat *Mary Joy*, Frank Cammish, better known in Filey and Scarborough as Frankie Dyer. Frank was a veteran of the fishing world, a true professional of the old school who had been at sea since he was a boy. He had learned his craft, his skills, in the old yawls and cobbles, where catches were made by strict adherence to the annual cycles of fish movement, to long tried and trusted methods as much as to plain old-fashioned hard work. As to the *Mary Joy*, she was a keelboat, typical of her kind and to be seen in any of the East Coast fishing harbours from Wick to Lowestoft. The *Mary Joy* had been built at Anstruther on the Firth of Forth in 1934, 48 feet long, carvel built of all-timber construction with a Kelvin diesel engine as her heart, she had been through all the fevers from trawling to driftnetting, potting to lining, in all weathers and through all seasons.

It was a Tuesday, as I remember, in mid-September, a foggy but mild morning that took me through the streets of old Filey towards what was then Dowson's Garage corner. There at just after 3.30 a.m. I met Frank and his crew as they waited for their lift through to Scarborough. Matt Cappleman, Paul Robinson and William Wright, better known in Filey as Matty Tatt, Paul Hobby and Dont, respectively. Like Frankie Dyer they were all in their sixties now; veterans, at sea since boyhood, they had done and seen it all and still survived. These four Filonians would be augmented by a further two from Scarborough, Jock Addison and Harry Moon, both no doubt making their way through Scarborough to the *Mary Joy*. For all of them it was just another day, a day like any other, though maybe relieved by having a guest aboard as a source of humour, for I surely had no idea at all as to just what I had let myself in for on that memorable day. Eventually the van arrived and we got aboard. A short journey, mostly made in silence, brought us to Scarborough harbour and the day began. At least it did for the crew, who with well-practiced art began by unloading the previous day's catch, clearing space below decks for the coming catch, including loading boxes of fresh herrings for bait, together with boxes of ice to keep whatever we hoped to catch cool and fresh for tomorrow's market.

It was a little after half past six when all was ready and we carefully, gingerly, let go the mooring ropes and eased our way from beside the harbour wall towards the West Pier, Seagate, and out towards the open sea. The fog was still hanging over the town and the south bay, and though the light was fast breaking it did little to relieve the dank gloom of the morning. Half a degree south of east was our course, and as the crew began to prepare the decks with baskets of longlines, *Mary Joy* came to life as the engine increased its roar and the screw bit deep into the long, slowly moving swells that rolled towards us from the dawn of the morning.

My prime concern that morning was to gain my sealegs, to become accustomed to a movement of a deck that was much different to that of my own boat; no matter what kind of sea state the day may produce, I must not get seasick. I reasoned that if I kept above decks, my eyes upon the horizon (when it eventually became visible), then I had a very good chance indeed. For 90 minutes I stayed on deck, walking around it, looking at the neatly laden baskets of longlines, their woven tops lined with shiny hooks, watching Matty Tatt, Dont and Paul Hobby preparing the herrings by cutting them diagonally from back to belly to produce neat strips of bait that could be readily put upon the hooks. Eventually they finished and invited me to join them for breakfast. Well aware of the probable implications of that invitation, I reluctantly accepted. The fo'c'sle was much as I had expected it to be; a haze of blue tobacco smoke pervaded the scene like the fog that still surrounded the *Mary Joy*, augmented by smoke from the pot-bellied iron stove that wheezed and crackled slowly into a growing warmth. For ten minutes I survived, until the biggest frying pan I have ever seen before or since began to cook breakfast for all the crew at the same time. Fatty bacon, large sausages, black pudding, mushrooms, a bit of liver, a sliced onion, and several eggs all vying for both heat and space to cook, threatened to overcome me, and I fled back on deck for some fresh air.

It was now two hours since we had left Scarborough and still the fog persisted, with visibility some 200 yards on each quarter. At this point Frank called out for Matt to come on deck and asked him if we had arrived yet. Matt duly obliged and came up onto the deck, walked towards the bow, and took a long and deep sniff. He paused for a moment, sniffed again and looked back towards the wheelhouse.

'No, Frank, not yet,' said Matt, and with that he returned below decks to the last of his breakfast.

To say that this little scene bewildered me had to be the understatement of the year. I made my way towards the bridge and looked inside for charts, scale rules, dividers or anything else that would indicate how we had got where we were after two hours of steaming on this very foggy morning. But there was nothing at all upon the chart desk and Frank, seeing my perplexed look, merely smiled at me and remained silent. The next time Matt appeared he did so without being called, and as before made his way forward up to the bow and again repeated the same exercise.

'Aye, we're nearer now. Put 'er over to starboard. Aye, some four hundred yards ah reckon.'

I stood in silent disbelief at this charade, which I was quite certain was being put on for my benefit, and had nothing whatever to do with where we were supposed to be heading. Frank duly put the helm over and *Mary Joy* swung slowly to starboard, the bow lifting leisurely to the soft swell that had persisted all the morning. For some two minutes Matt kept on sniffing the air, nodding each time and looking back towards Frank as he did so.

'Aye, we're here, this be t' spot reet enough.' And with that he turned towards me and smiled, and I was as sure as I could be that it was an act put on to mislead me into believing it was for real. It was to be many years before I found out the truth behind Matt's unusual behaviour.

Within minutes all was action and activity, baskets of lines were put into order, the boxes of herring strip were made ready and the day began in earnest. First of all the danbuoys with their anchors that marked the beginning of the lines to be shot were tossed over the side, and then followed the lines. Each basket contained 300 bare hooks attached to the main fishing line by means of a snood or trace of line 3 feet long, each hook and snood being separated from the next by 3 yards of line. With each basket of line connected to another there had to have been no mistake when the line was 'caved' (laid) in the baskets; the hooks, snoods and line must flow from each basket with mechanical ease and then from basket to basket until every basket of line and hooks had been shot.

The baiting of the line was an art unto itself. The trick was to pick up the hook with one hand, throw the herring strip onto the hook with sufficient force to push the point and barb through the skin and flesh of the strip so as to hold it firm, but not so strongly as to break down the strip into a mushy pulp that would not stay on the hook. Then the baited hook was tossed over the side and the exercise repeated again until all the hooks, snoods and longline contained in each basket had been shot. It took two men who stood facing each other to shoot the line; it was an exercise in skill of the highest order as with each yard of line shot the strain and pull upon the remaining unshot line increased. Any hook not properly laid upon the rim of the creel would foul up the shooting of the line for sure, and with potentially hazardous consequences. As each basket of line was shot the boxes of herring or new baskets of line were moved into position, and the shoot continued until at last the final basket arrived and eventually the last 100 yards of line.

It was at this point that the first badly laid hook appeared, and Matt was the one that had the misfortune to pick up the mislaid hook. As I watched, the hook reared up quickly and fiercely, breaking free of Matt's fingers, and with one sudden plunge drove downward as Matt's hand reached out to grab the offending snood. He was too late.

The hook drove into the flat palm of his hand and with equal speed pulled Matt round and began to drag him towards the ship's side and overboard. Matt, no slight man, was rotund and heavy, but it mattered not whether he weighed 20 stone or a mere 10, the force acting upon the hook was 9 miles long and irresistible. He was pulled off his feet, his hooked hand being swung inevitably towards the sea and Matt with it. I looked on with shocked disbelief, for it all appeared to be taking place in slow motion, with stilted unreal movements but with a deadly significance that was rapidly becoming a reality. As Matt continued to move outwards like some spinning top, Dont, standing behind him, grabbed his collar and pulled Matt towards himself. As Matt fell, half towards the sea and half towards Dont, Dont grabbed at a long carving knife that had been stuck into the cabin wall by his right hand. The knife, stuck into the wheelhouse wall alongside the spot where the lines are shot, and left there for this very purpose, came free and with one long sweeping curve Dont slashed at the hook snood, cutting it clean through in one go. Matt stumbled back into the boat and crashed against the cabin wall. Dont, still holding onto Matt's collar, caught him and passed him back towards the stern of the boat where I stood open-mouthed.

Matt, now standing upright again, walked towards me and extended his hand. 'C'mon, Norman. Let's have it out.'

'Matt! You must be kidding! That hook is buried to the bend of the hook. I could never get that out, that's a hospital job that is!'

'Norman, get it out. There's a lot of work to be done today and I can't do it wit a bleedin' hook stuck in me hand!'

I looked at him with disbelief. I doubted he could be serious, but Matt's attitude said he surely was, and that he was determined to have the hook out. Simply, I prayed. I prayed very hard.

'Matt, I do not want to do this at all, not at any price, but I shall have a go if you insist.'

'C'mon Norman, stop pratting about, get it out,' replied Matt.

I carefully took hold of the bend of the hook that was visible. To my amazement there was no blood, but the palm already looked bruised and swollen.

'Ready, Matt?'

'Aye,' replied Matt.

With one quick twist of my hand I reversed the hold of the barb and then I pulled the hook upwards. The hook flew free. Matt smiled and walked away, and finding a bucket of seawater, thrust his hand in and swilled it about, wringing his hands dry to finish. For Matt this incident was just another hazard, another price to be paid to work in this most arduous of jobs. Despite the hole in his palm Matt continued to work all day long, including the hauling of the lines, all of which must have exacerbated the pain in his hand. The next day he was back at sea as if nothing had happened, and as far as he was concerned, nothing had happened.

The lines now shot, it was time for lunch, to wait and to give the 9 miles of line with over 5,000 hooks time to fish; time for the Turbot, which were our prime target, to find the bait and take it. For about an hour we waited, eating, smoking, doing odd jobs as *Mary Joy* gently rose and fell to the easing swell, the fog of the morning thinning now, and the first shafts of sunlight breaking the gloom.

The hauling of the lines is no easy matter and even with a mechanical hauler to help it is still a matter of strength, and work for a fit man. The first few hooks were as they had been shot, the bait untouched, then the longline jinked and went out of alignment to the slowly moving track of the *Mary Joy*, and up through the dark green of the water came a long white shape as the first fish of the day came to the surface, a Cod of 12 lb, grey-backed with dappled grey and white flanks flecked with spots of gold, a far cry indeed from the dull grey creatures that one sees upon a fishmonger's slab. It was well hooked and Jock Addison, who had taken first stint upon the hauler, lifted the fish from the water and swung it up and onto the deck.

For ten minutes Cod, with the odd smattering of Haddock and Tub Gurnard, came steadily to the deck, where Paul Hobby and myself dealt with them, putting them into boxes prior to their being stacked below decks.

'Gaff!' cried out Jock.

Harry Moon who was in attendance at the hauler moved to the deck edge, a long-handled gaff in his right hand. I went aft of the hauler and peered down into the clear green depths to see a Turbot as big as a serving tray moving up towards the boat side. As I looked I could see it was well hooked, and for a moment wondered why Jock had called for the gaff for he had had no problem in lifting good fish up onto the deck without the use of the gaff. After all, a mistake in the gaffing of the fish could either lose the fish completely by knocking it off the hook, or the gaff itself if clumsily handled could go into the flank of the fish, damaging the flesh and so reducing its value. But Jock's call was for a completely different reason, for as the hooked Turbot came ever closer to the boat's side there, swimming up with the hooked fish, was its mate, which had followed either out of curiosity or by instinct. Harry waited till the hooked Turbot was almost directly under the hauler, Jock stopped hauling, the hooked fish continued swimming alongside the slowly moving boat while its mate came up through the water, and ever closer to its mate. Harry made no mistake: the gaff took the curious Turbot directly, and as Harry lifted the startled fish from the water, hauled up onto the deck came the hooked Turbot.

'Two for the price of one, eh Paul?' I remarked, still amazed at what I had just seen.

'Its commonplace, Norman, happens all the time when you're after Turbot', said Paul.

So the day progressed and the fish continued to come, the Turbot regularly and in pairs, all of a size between 15 and 20 lb, with the odd fish well over 20 lb. All the Turbot were deep-bodied, firm-fleshed, white-bellied and with that wondrous mottled sandy brown back, a genius of camouflage design. There would be a run of bare hooks which would suddenly be stopped by the appearance of a fish, usually

115

a Cod, and then a few more hooks later the Turbot would come, singly or in pairs. Spurdogs, the odd Woof (a much more attractive name than Catfish which the Woof really is) and then a further surprise as large scallops had taken the herring strip baits. Scallops, known locally as 'Queenies', did not last long for they were a delicacy much loved by all the crew: no sooner were the scallops lifted aboard than they were taken from the hook, slit open and eaten.

By mid-afternoon, with almost all lines now hauled, the *Mary Joy* sailed out into the sunlight. As I looked out and away to port and to starboard there, coming out of the banks of sea fog came other keelboats, all on parallel courses to the *Mary Joy*. They too had been after the Turbot and I wondered if they had done as well as we had. By all the rules they should have had at least as good a day as us; after all, most of them were much better equipped than was the *Mary Joy*. With Decca Navigators, and the latest in technology of echo-meters (a form of underwater radar, an electronic fish finder, which though still in its early days was still very effective), all a far cry from a plain compass and the masthead radar reflector which was all the equipment *Mary Joy* sported. The beginnings of a breeze rippled the sea's surface and as I looked forward beyond the bow I could see the flags of the danbuoys that marked the end of *Mary Joy*'s longlines, and with them the end of the fishing. It had been a good day, and as it turned out *Mary Joy* had beaten all comers, a tribute to old-fashioned skills and know-how.

Today that day is memory. The *Mary Joy* was lost at sea in 1968, and Frankie Dyer, Matty Tatt, Paul Robinson and Jock Addison are now, sadly, no longer with us, while Dont enjoys a quiet retirement in a residential nursing home overlooking Filey Bay. The North Sea is now but a shadow of its former self, and no week goes by without the ever growing threat of a ban on at least Cod fishing, if not a ban on all fishing, as the stocks of fish reach desperate new lows. If the fishing philosophies of Frank, Matt, Paul and Dont had been followed and fishing had been governed and carried out as they practiced it, such bans would have been the stuff of nightmares and not a growing reality. Instead, fishing techniques that despoil and destroy both the fish stocks and the grounds that hold the fish are rigorously followed and applied. Whereas longline fishing was and still is a conservation form of fishing, the trawl and trammel net kill the stocks indiscriminately, and where the beam trawl is used the grounds too suffer such damage that they cannot be fished again for a long time, if at all. Why do we still go down that road of exploitation and excess until it is all but impossible to go back and rectify the situation?

As for Matty Tatt and his sniffing, it was several years before I discovered that it had been no charade, but a vital act of fish location. One morning as dawn broke I was fishing for Mackerel from Filey Brigg. As the light increased I was suddenly assaulted by a strong smell of fish that came from nowhere. I looked at the sea, and to my amazement within a few yards of the scar's edge was a huge shoal of herring, 40 yards long and 5 yards wide. It slowly swam along before me, a pale luminescent lime-green cloud of fish. As it slowly disappeared from my view, so too did the smell.

When I saw Matt that evening and told him of my belated discovery, he laughed, but was not prepared to add anything at all.

'Norman,' he said, 'one day I'll tell you how we hand-fed Tunny from *Mary Joy*.' And he chuckled in his inimitable way, and I was left wondering how long it would be before I found out the secret of the hand-fed Tunny. Sadly, I never did.

The Casting Competition

The third notable event of that year, 1963, the Casting Competition, happened on a beautiful warm Saturday evening when I decided to go for a walk. My aim was to go onto Filey Brigg and see if anyone was fishing for Mackerel (a near certainty in early July, except I may not know any of the local anglers involved) and end up at Foords for a pint. It was a pleasant walk onto the Brigg, Carr Naze, and I arrived at the top of the first security ladder feeling more than a little warm. The first security ladder stands directly above and behind Green Rock, a local hotspot for Mackerelling, where a dozen rods, mostly made up of people I knew and all of them in their late teens or early twenties, were trying hard for the elusive Mackerel.

I climbed down the ladder and sat down on the edge of the rock steps that lead onto the flat scar that is Green Rock, and began to watch. Despite the efforts of all involved it was apparent that there were no Mackerel, at least this evening, which came as a disappointment to me obviously as to go Mackerelling had always been an exciting way to spend a summer evening. After about an hour of effort two anglers began to argue about the fishing, and particularly about casting. They put down their spinning gear and from behind a rock outcrop produced a rod; attached was a multiplier reel.

'A multiplier!' My instant private reaction to the reel was of scorn. In my (then) closed mind a multiplier was as much use as a chocolate teapot. To my mind that evening a Scarborough reel was the only reel to fish any kind of rough ground; a fixed spool reel was AOK as long as it was used over clean ground or a beach, and certainly of no use anywhere else.

The two young men were Fred Hall and John Addis, who I knew, but not that well, from before my move to Leeds seven years before. They tackled up the rod. The rod itself was of interest: it was a stainless steel tubed and split-cane-clad sea rod 11 feet long, and at the time quite popular with sea anglers in the area. The reel was a Penn Surfmaster laden with 20 lb b.s. monofilament line; the attached 5-oz lead gave the whole outfit a balanced look.

Without further ado, John and Fred moved to the edge of Green Rock and after a further bit of banter it was agreed that Fred would cast first. How they were to decide who had cast the furthest was not decided.

'Hey, Nav,' said John, 'you decide, right?'

'Me?' I queried.

'Aye, you,' said Fred.

So it was. But it was not the the distance that grabbed me by the throat. It was the tackle used and the ease of using it. Neither John nor Fred broke the magic 100 yards, they cast about 80 to 90 yards and there was nothing between them, but to hear Fred go on you would think that Fred was outdistancing John by miles, which he certainly was not doing. They had both been using multipliers for some time, their techniques were much the same, both as simple as one would imagine, no thought given as to drop length nor the length of the swing and the timing necessary to get the greatest possible energy release. The ease with which both of them got the lead out and away as compared to the usual style of casting required when using a Scarborough reel looked so easy, so straightforward, that I was hooked.

To cast with a Scarborough reel you have to turn your back on the target you are aiming at, which if you think about it means that your technique, to hit that target, must be near faultless; and few Scarborough reel users were that good. If you have got everything right, as well as your timing, the lead will go 70 or 80 yards if you are good, 60 to 70 yards being the average.

The similarity of this technique to the 'pendulum cast' that materialised some years later is self-evident, but all the techniques of casting that would fill our thinking and change much of angling were still to come. I was only aware of what I had seen, and feeling the effects of this demonstration upon me, I had a lot to think about. Just what was I to do as far as my future sea fishing life was concerned?

I left the Brigg with John and Fred, the whole walk being filled with questions about the rod and reel, particularly: had either John or Fred done any good, fishing-wise, with this new tackle? Their answer was 'Yes!' but not enough to shout about, and anyway to use this kind of tackle, especially a multiplier, in Filey and its environs was to risk a deal of verbal abuse: 'Is tha using a glass rod an' all?' Fibreglass ('glass') rods were just coming onto the market and were treated with scorn and contempt by many local anglers whose criticisms implied that the rods, being 'made of glass', would shatter if wrongly used or if they fell over onto a rock scar! This level of contempt I could understand, and within a couple of years I was to experience a great deal of such abuse when I used a multiplier and a 'glass' rod to fish the Brigg and other local locations.

I was not quite penniless, with my new job and better salary, but the balance at the month's end was really not enough to go out and buy new fishing tackle, so I had to use what I already had and experiment with a multiplier. The first multiplier I had was a second-hand Ocean City reel I bought from another of my fishing friends, Geoff 'Nags' Jenkinson. After this reel there were several other reel purchases until a degree of competence was achieved, only after using up many hundreds of yards of monofilament line, all ruined as a result of numerous backlashes as I tried to master a multiplier. I ended up in late 1965 with a Pfleuger Sea Queen, bought new, and this proved to be an excellent multiplier, with a good casting control system and, most important of all, it was reliable and robust.

My aim was to be able to cast it well in all circumstances, like on fine summer days, freezing days when you could not feel your fingers, at night particularly, on unsure footings like wet, seaweed-covered boulders, in a gale … essentially, to be able to use the reel in any location, in any circumstances where such a reel could be used effectively.

At first my rod was a Martin James Heavy Duty Keelson. I had bought this rod in the early 1960s and there were two rods in the range, one called 'Light', the other 'Heavy Duty' (HD). Of course being a staid old-fashioned Tory I opted for the HD version: a great mistake. It was 11 feet 6 inches long, and it was indeed HD: it was very heavy. It had all the characteristics and the flexibility of a poker, and casting with it was hard work. I fixed the reel 28 inches above the butt end of the rod and clamped the reel to the bare fibreglass of the rod with reel clamps to hold it firmly in position. Despite my very best efforts I never threw a lead further than 90 yards, but in the event the need to be able to cast further never arose in practice, as I did catch fish.

Then in July 1965 in *Creel* magazine, a Hardy advertisement displayed its new sea angling rod, the Longbow. Designed by Les Moncrieff, a Kentish man who had become famous for his catches of Cod, especially from Dungeness. This was his second effort at a radical rod design. Mr Moncrieff, being an engineer by profession, designed a rod with a reverse tapered butt. Essentially, the rod butt tapered in diameter, from the reel seat down to the butt of the rod. The concept was that such a taper within the rod itself and below the fulcrum point (that is, the reel seating) would eliminate the snatch out of the act of casting and thus reduce significantly the threat of overruns and backlashes that were commonplace on casting on a conventionally designed rod.

Mr Moncrieff's first attempt at this radical new concept of rod design was the Martin James Springheel, a rod that I only became aware of some time later; it was one hell of a rod, but you had to be at least 6 feet 4 inches tall and built like a Colossus if you were to get the very best out of the rod and its design. I bought the Longbow for 19 guineas (£19.95) and took delivery a few days later. I took it immediately to my local playing fields, full of expectancy and almost a-tingle with excitement.

It did look good, though I was not impressed with the ceramic and moveable butt ring! I tackled it up with my Pflueger Sea King multiplier with 22 lb b.s. monofilament line and a 5-oz bomb lead.

Then I discovered that the distance of the reel from the bottom of the rod was at least 42 inches; that meant with my modest arm length it would be impossible for me to cast with the rod with my left hand at the butt and my right hand controlling the reel. So it proved. No matter how I tried I could not cast properly unless my left hand was at least a foot above the butt.

Nonetheless, after my inflexible poker, the Keelson, I was greatly impressed; all I had to do was to sort out the butt length. In the event I got in touch with Hardy's who offered to cut back the butt and refit the black rubber grips for a modest fee. I agreed, the rod butt was dispatched to Alnwick, and two weeks later the rod was returned duly modified.

For me, and for any angler of average height, the ideal distance of the reel seat to the butt of the rod is 28 inches. After some discussion and on hearing Hardy's advice this was the distance we settled on, and for me it was ideal; it worked, and will for everyone of average height. If you are taller and your arms are proportionately that bit longer, that length of 28 inches will need to be longer. If, of course, you are a 'pendulum caster' with the reel set just above the rod's butt, then none of this applies.

The return to the playing fields was this time a resounding success, with most of my casts passing the 100 yards mark, and straight with it. I was delighted and remained so until some six years later I changed my much-loved Longbow for an ABU 464, but more of that later.

The winter fishing of 1963/64 was for the most part a disaster. No matter how hard I tried, fishing locally for the most part, I had next to nothing. My technique for digging bait (in sand) had suffered badly from seven years of modest living, and I missed a good many worms by either being not fit enough, or not quick enough, in my digging.

There is a real art in the digging of lugworm. When you see it done by someone who knows what he is about it is much like watching any skilled artisan doing what he does best, easily and with seemingly little effort. I am not sure this is the place to describe the ways and means of how to dig this most precious of baits. For starters, there are two types of lugworm that the sea angler seeks. In a perfect world it will always be the lugworm that is known generally as a 'yellowtail', with an all but black body, which can be as long as 12 inches, but ideally 6 inches long. These lugs, known locally as 'gullies', are the very best of lug bait, nothing compares and so they are sought feverishly and with very serious intent. The other lugworm species are known as 'blasties'; they can be up to 8 inches long but they are intrinsically a much softer, more tender bait, and though they do fish they cannot compare with a gullie.

The task is of great importance; you measure the quality of lugworm as a bait by its ability to go onto a hook, its ability to stay on the hook, especially through the power of the cast, and its ability to act as a bait once it is in the position chosen to fish. Without these qualities you might as well stay at home.

You need a bucket and a potato fork if you are to dig lug in sand. If you are to dig in a mixture of mud and sand, or mud alone (as in an estuary), a drain trenching spade is best. Of course there was available in the mid-1960s a proper 'graving' fork; named after its style of bait digging, you dug a 'grave', a hole up to 3 feet deep and as long as 4 or 5 feet in length, essentially a 'grave'. So, 'graving', is the name given on the Yorkshire coast for the act of digging bait. Once upon a time it was possible to dig yellowtailed black lugworm from a trench three spits wide and three spits deep that was continous in its length, and which on occasion would have produced several score or more of absolutely perfect lug. But serious overdigging of lug has destroyed such beds of lugworm and now it is a matter of digging individual worms. Provided of course that you can find a suitable beach and bait bed.

The alternative to the trench was to dig a single hole; this is *the* way for almost all digging of lug on sandy beaches. Anyway, an alternative to the potato fork, as I said earlier was the 'graving' fork, which was in effect a three-pronged fork, with about 1 ¾ inches gap between the tynes. Each tyne was about 10 inches long, with an arrow-pointed end; the shaft of ash wood was 60 inches long and very strong. It was also a very heavy fork and you had to be physically fit and strong to use it to its best, but then you had to be fit and strong to go digging bait in the first place.

It is imperative that the tool used is strong in every aspect of its design, otherwise you will be having to buy a new tool on a regular basis. Anyway, you now have the tools and are ready in every way to go dig your own bait. Then you have to find a place where you can find the lugworm and there are no local byelaws to stop you digging for the bait. Providing everything is AOK, come the next spring tide and low water you get yourself onto this beach about half an hour before low water itself and begin to look for the tell-tale casts of lugworm. The casts can be anywhere: close by the low water line or 50 yards further up the beach. Once found, your first spit will be about 12 to 14 inches away from the cast on its seaward side. Not too narrow a dig; not too wide either, especially if the sand is wet: it is very heavy.

Dig purposely, no haste, clearing the hole of loose sand as you proceed. If you do not clear this loose sand it will impede your digging for sure as you go deeper into the sand and backwards. You must keep looking keenly onto the face of the sand you are cutting into; eventually you will see a perfectly formed hole appear on the face of the spit, about half and inch or more in diameter, with a touch of water at its rim. Now you must concentrate, try very hard not to rush, but continue as you had up to the moment that you spotted the hole. Deeper now, you must dig behind and get underneath that deepest spit of sand; if you have done it properly as you lift out the spit the worm's tail will be visible in that spit or visible in the bottom of the exposed hole.

To dig a 'blastie' is a much easier task. Find the cast, then find the circular blowhole and dig from blow hole to cast. Do not dig more than a couple of spits deep, for the worm lies in a U-shaped tunnel with its head towards the blowhole and its tail towards the cast.

Remember too that as you dig your lugworm it is all but certain that you will find other probable baits, namely Sand Eels and razorfish (called 'warfish' in Filey). Both work well, especially warfish;

125

with this bait there is a bonus in that you can preserve the bait by keeping it in salt, which comes very useful when your lugworm is in very short supply.

Having got your worm the next problem is to keep it alive. I never went along with the school of thought that said 'Gut 'em and keep in paper in the fridge'! The best material I ever found for keeping lug alive in for days was deepwater seaweed, creamy white in colour and found after a big sea at the high water mark, but you need to look for it: it's never readily available. Wet it so that all of it is damp, scatter your worms in it and put the bucket in a cool place. Bingo! Now go fishing.

One night in early December 1964, Martin Scotter, David Morton and I were fishing Ling Rock on the back of Filey Brigg. Despite the best of bait, ideal conditions, a gentle lift to the sea and a moonlit night, the three rods did not produce a single bite. This was not the first time we had gone off full of hopes and been disappointed. The result of this was that Martin said that we should give the Holderness coast a try, particularly Skipsea. The conversation continued in our local pub, the Foords, for to fish at Skipsea meant that a whole new ball game of fishing had to be addressed.

In those days if you found a fishing catalogue, the sea fishing section would, if it existed at all, would be barely a page or two on A5 sheets showing a rod and, more often than not, a Nottingham reel adapted for the sea angler. Today, a sea angler's catalogue can be 100 pages plus of the most detailed list and illustrations of the very best of sea fishing tackle, and the range available ... wow! In the mid-1960s this would have been beyond our wildest dreams; anyone starting out today cannot have any kind of excuse for failure, nor for not having the best of tackle, save lack of personal funds. (Let us forget for the moment the destruction of the sea fisheries!) That night in Foords we made a list of the tackle that we would need to fish the Holderness coastline properly. It was not a long list: grip leads were at the top of our list, everything else was secondary to that problem.

And a problem it was for some years. We solved the problem then in a simplistic and very basic way: we used a flat, fish-shaped lead of 5 oz and hammered two 4-inch nails through it, and that was it. There was no thought as to the aerodynamics of the lead, nor did any other ingenious thought process come upon us that would improve this most primitive grip lead. There was a memorable tale to the end of this problem.

In 1968, or thereabouts, there was a report in the angling press that Don's of Edmunton had designed a quick-release grip lead. A spokesman for the company was reported as saying it was still undergoing development. So I wrote to the company, crossed their palm with silver, and asked if they could simply sketch out exactly how the system worked. To their very great credit they did just that, and by return of post came a small, simple sketch of their idea.

At 6.30 p.m. on a Friday night I showed the sketch to a very select few of my fishing friends; Noddy Bannister asked to borrow it and said he'd be back in a couple of hours, and he was. In a most dramatic manner two hours later Noddy returned to Foords, and after getting through the crowded public bar to where we were all sat, he took a small packet from his pocket and proceeded to open it. Out onto the drinks table there fell a lead identical to the ones we used for casting tournaments, but this time it had been modified so that there were two stainless steel wires suitably bent and shaped and held in position with an elastic band, which in turn was tied to a small nylon link tied to the lead itself. We were speechless. It was so simple! We adopted that design immediately and for a long time it was our secret; until, of course, the secret was out and quick-release grip leads were everywhere. It was a very generous thing that Don's of Edmunton did for us, and it is still much appreciated.

It was a Saturday at the end of November when the three of us got to Skipsea. I had never been there before, and having parked the car on the side of the road that led to the beach, I walked to the cliff edge, extremely curious as to what I would find. In those days the road turned at right-angles 20 yards from the cliff edge, then the road went on south for another 200 yards or so, fronting the gardens and the beach bungalows that stretched away to our right, ending where the cliffs met a small dyke that drained the fields behind the bungalows themselves.

The beach that day was only about 80 yards wide, and quite steep with two broken and badly damaged World War II concrete blockhouses, the larger one away to my left and the other barely showing above the sand. There was a typical south-easterly sea running, modest waves with narrow flat tables of water between each wave, producing what looked like a series of white-edged steps that went all the way out to the grey, ill-defined horizon beyond. Such conditions, we came to learn, were as near perfect for 'Cod bashing' on the north end of the Holderness coast as you could ever wish for, but as I stood and looked at it for the first time I did not know that then. It being only an hour after low water it was impossible to 'read the beach', a skill which then we had only the vaguest clue about, but its importance we would soon learn.

After climbing down the short cliff path of steep muddy steps, we decided to set up our camp by the remains of the smaller of the two concrete blockhouses. Tackle was simple. My Keelson rod, the Pfleuger Sea King multiplier, loaded with 22 lb b.s. monofilament line, a fish-shaped lead with two nails to act as an anchor on a 26 lb b.s. trace, a size 6/0 bronze hook on a 18-inch trace, the set-up all fixed to a brass buckle swivel with the main line attached to the other end. Bait was, as it was almost every time we went 'Cod bashing' down Holderness, lugworm. Some was freshly dug that morning and some we had left over from our abortive trip during the week; it was excellent bait, and so it proved.

From the first cast right up to high water when we had to get off the beach completely, we had fish almost every cast. They were not big, all about 2 to 3lb Codling, but they went very well despite the 5-oz anchor that every fish had to fight as well as ourselves as they were reeled in. On leaving the beach because of the height of the tide, we were determined to continue to fish, and had set up our 'basecamp' on the road when a local walking past us with his dog quietly pointed out that we should adjourn to the pub and come back in about 90 minutes, 'Cos this 'ere beach fishes best on t' ebb.'

That was what we decided to do, and we ended up at the Board, which over the next ten years of our fishing lives proved to be a very popular drinking house for us at the end of our days out. Just over an hour later we were back on the beach and fishing as before. The quality of the fishing continued but we caught nothing bigger than we had on the flooding tide. We fished on for another two hours before the rain that had begun with a whisper had turned into a regular downpour, and with that we'd had enough and called it a day.

After so many blank days fishing from the rock scars of Filey and Scarborough, to go to a new location, a beach at that, and catch as we had that Saturday in 1964 was a revelation. It is difficult not to get the day out of proportion to its importance; but as from that day on my whole attitude to sea fishing changed a great deal. I began to read everything that was available to read in those days, but that is not saying very much: the *Angling Times*, *Angler's Mail* and the unique *Creel* magazine, and that was it, no more instructive reading was available. There were other reads but they did not amount to much in our lives. We discussed, we argued, we actually began to go and practice our casting techniques, and the distances we began to achieve, though never prodigious, were good enough to cater for every fishing situation we were likely to see.

One must remember that even had the choice of tackle available to us been as varied as today's, our incomes were such that we were unable to take advantage of it, and what we had, had to be enough. Rod design, particularly in materials available, was limited, carbon fibre was still some time in the future, and as for multipliers, these were almost entirely designed and made in the US of A. K.P. Morritt had brought out the Intrepid Surfcast fixed spool reel, ABU had the little 6000 Millionaire multiplier, but neither had an attraction for us. We looked upon the Surfcast as a 'mangle', unsuitable for the rough world of rock fishing and questionable in regard to beach fishing; the spool was not wide enough to hold sufficient line, or so we thought. The ABU was just too small and with a retrieve that was utterly inadequate. In truth I do not recall anyone in my then fishing world who ever mentioned either reel; it was a Penn or Ocean City for the most part, and I still used Pfleuger Sea Queen successfully enough not to want to change for change's sake.

Then, in the autumn of 1966, I was chosen to fish for Filey Brigg Angling Society in a match against Redcar SAC. Both Filey and the Redcar club were members of the Northern Federation of Sea Anglers and they ran a Knockout Competition every year; and so it was that Filey anglers travelled to Redcar to fish the first leg of that round. I was drawn to fish against the local tackle dealer, Harry Brough, who took me down onto the scars and runnels that flank the outer edge of Redcar Beach. I never had a bite, and Harry just one small Codling, but what made this night memorable was what Harry did after about an hour's uneventful fishing. He asked me how I found the Penn Squidder that I was using that night. I told him it was newly bought, and that this was its first outing, but so far it had performed well.

'Just watch this, Norman!' he said.

I turned to watch. Keeping my lamp on the ground near his feet so as not to spoil his night vision, I saw Harry turn his back to the sea, swing the lead out from his body and move into the act of casting he had adopted to use that night. But, as he bent into the cast, he suddenly took his hand off the multiplier and held the rod just by its butt, keeping the rod tip up and the whole rod pointing out into the night, following the path of the fast-disappearing lead. I saw the reel spool spin, saw the line begin to climb up from the spool leading towards an inevitable backlash, but it did not impede the spool's rotation one little bit. He had cast a lead out, at night, leaving control of the flying lead to the reel itself. Amazing. I was gobsmacked, I can tell you!

'How about that, then?' asked Harry as at last the lead hit the sea and he began to take up the slack line.

'Was it as long as your other casts?' I asked.

'Look for yourself!' and he pushed the rod and reel towards me. To my eyes the line appeared to have gone out as far as before because of the depth of empty spool showing in the light of my lamp.

'Hell! What kind of multiplier is that?' I asked.

'An ABU 9000, Norman, absolutely new to the UK and brilliant. Believe me, quite brilliant!'

You could not have had a better display as to what a reel can do than that shown by Harry that night. I asked many questions, such as what was the rate of line recovery; that it had a two-speed geared line recovery system amazed me, and since I did not fully appreciate what a geared two-speed system was, this only added to the glamour and mystery of the reel. Eventually I dared to ask how much it cost; not that it mattered, because I knew that as soon as I was able to I was going to have one. I did buy it, although I eventually would end up owning a dozen other sea fishing multipliers, most of them by ABU, and loved some of them dearly (the ABU 8000 being the very best of them all in my view); the 9000 was my first choice of reel for many years thereafter.

The match finished at ten o'clock that night and Filey lost. As I recall, I am sure that Redcar won the return match at Filey two weeks later, much to our embarrassment; not that it mattered to me as I had been unable to fish due to my work. Harry Brough's display made that night memorable beyond words, and I shall be ever grateful to Harry for both his hospitality on the night and his display of reel expertise.

There must be a postscript to this tale of reels, and one that is indeed worthy of report. K.P. Morritt produced a number of multipliers, probably the most popular being the Seastreak, which at one time seemed to be used by every other angler. The Morritt multiplier that I bought was a Fastback, and on delivery the spool would not move! In the event the two side plates that held the spool in position had been squeezed towards each other and all I had to do was realign them, which was easier said than done. But once restored to its proper alignment I used this reel for most of my rock and cliff fishing and it was an excellent performer. Its rate of retrieve was first class, something like 5 to 1, and it cast well too. Yes, it needed to be given TLC in maintenance and when casting, since there was no mechanical cast control system other than an educated thumb. For rough ground fishing it was first class, and if any rock angler out there is after a dependable, tough and reliable multiplier, this reel is highly recommended.

Between 1963 and 1968 was for me the learning curve. I fished Filey Brigg and everywhere locally, but predominately down the coast on Holderness, especially at Skipsea. It was during this period that sea angling went literally from the Dark Ages to the beginning of Enlightenment. By the late 1960s, fibreglass rods and even multiplier reels became almost commonplace on rock fishing venues which five years before would have been as rare a sight as rocking horse droppings. It was quite usual for some more elderly local angler to pass a derogatory comment about my tackle – a Longbow coupled with an ABU 9000 – as I made my way either onto the Brigg or down to Castey, or on to a cliff top.

And I was not alone in experiencing these verbal attacks, all my fishing friends went through the same, which usually went something like this: 'What's tha got there, then? Tha's never gannin' to fish 'ere wi' that, is tha?' As the day wore on and a fish or two were landed, sometimes the attitude did change; not a lot, I must admit, and not very often, but sometimes there came a softening of the initial aggression and even questions about the gear I was using. Nowadays, the latest in rod or reel design is the norm and there are some very able anglers who can cast as well and as far as anyone would wish, and certainly a great deal further than ever we did!

Come the summer days in the late 1960s, the Beverley Sea Angling Club began to organise casting tournaments in which the best casters in the UK would attend and show their casting skills, which always amazed us. Today, there can be no excuse for not being able to cast, and cast well. Tuition is available and videos or magazines offer advice and help to everyone so interested, and the record cast for a 150 gram lead is over 300 yards!

I do not want to get bogged down in arguments about the need to cast a country mile. Sometimes to be able to do so is a distinct advantage, but the skill of a sea angler is knowing where the fish are likely to lie, so being able to read the sea, and from those observations being able to read and know what the seabed is like, is in my view a much greater talent. Too many so-called sea anglers use casting techniques but have no ability whatever, and as a result are a clear danger on any fishing venue to every other angler within 300 yards. Too often I have seen anglers trying to cast using the pendulum casting style, and so inept have been their efforts that the lead has flown off and gone hurtling down the beach, knee-high, complete with baited hooks, to land eventually hundreds of yards further down the beach or rock scar. Thank goodness I never saw anyone injured by such incompetent casting techniques, but that was just good luck on the caster's part. There really can be no excuse whatever for such dangerous incompetency.

We went to see the tournaments, and as I have already said, we were amazed. There were trade stands on show with the latest tackle developments, and half a dozen really able casters 'doing their thing' with casts well in excess of 180 yards, which in those days was miraculous. Ever since that summer evening in 1963 when I watched John Addiss and Fred Hall having a casting competition on Green Rock, I have had an interest in everything to do with casting, be it rod design, the latest reels or even aerodynamically designed leads. In the late 1960s casting was (literally) really taking off, with rod design seemingly changing every other week, and ABU the reel manufacturer of the age having a reel to suit the growing challenge.

Today, the world record is a cast of 286.63 metres (313.46 yards) by a gentleman called Danny Moeskops, which is mind-blowing; the best cast any of my friends ever achieved was 163 yards by John Addiss, and for me 142 yards with my Longbow. But as far as I was concerned distance, though obviously very important, was not so vital. As long as I could get my bait out 80 to 100 yards when called for, achieve those lengths in daylight and at night, in rain or wind, and not put any bystanders' lives in jeopardy, I was content. I also hated 'leaders': the knot that connected the leader to the main line invariably caught bits of weed and it was always sufficient enough to block off the top ring of the rod, leaving you more times than not with a good fish still too far away from you to be landed safely, and the line well and truly jammed tight in that top ring. I fished with a main line, no leader, of usually 22 lb b.s., right through to the lead with hooks tied to 18 or 20 lb b.s. traces. And though I did on occasion throw off a lead, I generally had few problems, the result of a simple but effective casting style that I could rely on regardless of just about anything that nature and its conditions could throw at me.

I have two specific memories of those casting tournaments, and both involved Mr Peter Bagnell. We got to know Peter at these tournaments, not enough to be called lifelong buddies, but certainly enough to be able to call him by his first name and to chat informally and at length. Peter was ever friendly and helpful, as indeed he should have been as he was on a PR expedition for ABU and their rods and reels. Peter was, in particular, giving demonstrations of the then new ABU 484 sea fishing rod, which was radical in its design and concept.

As someone later remarked, 'It was like giving the keys of a Porsche sports car to a Model T Ford owner!' The 484 was built with a metal butt section, allied to a glass fibre rod of a rapid taper with a fine tip. The whole rod was completed with lightweight wire rings, which produced a rod of little weight and great power. It was without doubt a cracking rod, and the fine tip was great in giving excellent bite indication.

Peter, using his 'zoom' casting style, was putting in casts of over 180 yards seemingly with little effort, produced by a practised technique that left us speechless. Well, almost speechless. John, who had come to watch the tournament with the rest of us, commented that with Peter's build such casting results were inevitable. Peter was certainly a very strong and well-built man, in his prime, so such results could be said to be inevitable, especially with such a well-designed and purpose-built sea fishing rod. Nonetheless, what Peter did with that rod and a 5-oz lead was still a revelation, and the results fired our enthusiasm for our sport and all its branches that still lingers to this day.

The second memory is one that I think can now be told … On one visit to the Beverley Casting Tournament I saw a familiar face, a director of Hardy Bros, who was on a PR trip to the venue. After the usual greetings and pleasantries he suddenly thrust a rod, with reel and line attached, into my hands. 'Here, try this Norman. And let me have it back, OK?'

On inspection it was the new Hardy Bros sea fishing rod, the Tourney, designed by Les Moncrieff and as such a serious competitor to the ABU 484. We gave it a good going over: the same length as the 484, the same stiff butt, and well finished. What made it very difficult to use that day was that it had been set up with a Mitchell 624 boat reel complete with chromed brass spool filled with 35 lb b.s. main line and a 5-oz sinker! We found a quiet corner away from the stands and the many spectators and the four of us in turn tried our hand at casting the rod. I barely made 70 yards; of the other three John cast the furthest, 90 yards, and our collective opinion was that it was, if nothing else, a bit heavy even allowing for the reel.

As we were making our way back into the site area we literally bumped into Peter Bagnell. As soon as he saw the rod he was on it in an instant.

'Hi, fellahs! Eh, what's this then? Oh, let me guess: the new Hardy rod?'

'It is. They've called it the Tourney. Even allowing for the reel we think it's a bit on the heavy side.'

'Oh aye. C'mon, let's give it a go!' And with that he had hold of it and was off to the casting court.

On arrival at the court we found it was empty; what had been happening had now finished and everyone had gone off to lunch. Peter had by now moved into the casting point of the court, let the lead down to 5 or 6 feet below the rod tip, swung the lead away from him, and with one quck turn compressed the rod and then hit hard. Despite the fact that he was using a very large boat reel complete with large brass spool and heavy line, the cast we later discovered measured 160 yards!

No sooner had the lead landed than Peter turned towards me and threw the rod directly at me. As I reached out to grab the rod, Peter said just one word, 'Soft!' We were speechless. With that Peter turned from the court and went back into the showground for his lunch. We duly set about carefully retrieving the cast line, walking down the court towards the lead, buried hard and fast, 6 inches in the ground. The only thing said was, 'He threw that 160 yards with a bloody boat reel!'

We gave back the rod as we had received it to Hardy Bros, with never a word save 'Thank you!' Whatever Peter Bagnell did with his unexpected treat we never did learn, nor did we expect to; as for how well Hardy Bros did with the Tourney rod, only they really know. ABU had a staggering success with their 484, of that there can be little doubt.

There is a footnote to casting, and that is that in my experience the sea angler should never forget that when rock fishing the ability to cast well is a great asset, but that more fish have been caught from 'beneath the feet of the angler' than well off. Remember, too, that until the arrival of monofilament line, sea anglers used lines that today they would not be seen using if their lives depended on it, but at the time these were the only lines readily available. Dolphin Cuttyhunk, a treated cotton line, was one such line and there were others, but none of them aided casting. If an angler could cast over 70 yards with that kind of line, generally speaking he had to be a 7-foot, 18-stone giant! The average cast for the normal human being using such a line was 50 yards at best, and it was from that length of cast that 99 per cent of fish were caught on rocky venues.

Dungeness and Skipsea

Much to my chagrin I kept no diary of my fishing life between 1963 and 1968. I was extremely busy at work, having left my Scarborough employ to be re-employed by the firm which had trained me and for which I had worked until 1963. Now, my home was my office and my work was over much of the North Riding and Teesside. Nonetheless, it is certain that over this period I, together with Fred Hall, Martin Scotter and Noddy Bannister, particularly fished Filey and environs, but especially Skipsea whenever we could get there, and with growing success and know-how.

During the 1960s sea fishing, which had been popular with relatively few people, began to grow, and with the advent of sea angling reports in a growing number of publications it began to become an even more popular pastime. Very much at the forefront of this growth were two angling hotspots: Dungeness in Kent and Lowestoft and adjoining beaches in Norfolk. Two anglers in particular became ever more well known, essentially for their prodigious catches of Cod: these two anglers were Fred Williams of Yarmouth and Les Moncrieff of Kent. Dungeness became the place to visit, even if you lived up on the Yorkshire coast 250 miles from the place.

In late November 1967 Martin Scotter, David Morton and myself made our first visit, which was memorable for the fish seen and seen caught. We hired a Commer Caravanette which had definitely seen better days, and to add insult to injury had a knackered battery that caused us continual headaches throughout the time we had it on hire. The weather was typical late November, frost and snow, which added to the variety of the week and which at times scared us with the intensity of the frost.

One night in a pub car park in Romney was the only time in my life that I have heard a tree crack from the intensity of the frost. Whilst parking on the shingle near the Dungeness lighthouse we saw the inside of the van frozen to such an extent that we did not think it would ever defrost!

Our problem was that we had come all this way to fish Dungeness and to us that meant fishing the famous Point and its 'boil' of current and tide which was visible 100 yards off the Point. This spot held fish which to us were fish to dream about. On arrival we found that we could not get near the Point; it was full of anglers and rods, all with tents and other forms of shelter, and most had been long established. This meant we had a choice: to fish east of the point, which to our eyes looked to hold shallower waters, or to fish west of the Point, which was probably deeper water. We opted for the west side. It was all to no avail because we never had a bite. By late Tuesday we were so disappointed at our lack of success that we were considering leaving Dungeness and looking elsewhere.

On the Wednesday morning we were fishing about 100 yards west of the Point and again, despite our best efforts, we were fishless. Then 150 yards further west than we were, there arrived a party of six anglers. The way they arrived and set up their camp must have struck some kind of chord with me because I found myself watching their activities with interest. They had been fishing for about 20 minutes when there was a shout and one angler was seen to be involved with a good fish: his rod was curved over steeply. I admit that my curiosity got the better of me and I grabbed up our gaff and ran along the shingle beach to see the action, for by the look of it this was a good fish and we'd not even seen a fish yet.

By the time I got there it was obvious that this was a good fish and it was giving the angler a hard time, pulling him ever closer to the sea's edge, his reel whining every now and again as the fish took line against a seemingly hard-set clutch.

Looking around me I realised that all six of the anglers were elderly, certainly over 60 years old or more.

'Come for a look-see?' said the angler closest to where I stood.

'Aye. We've been here since Friday and this is the first fish we've seen caught and my curiosity overtook my natural reticence,' I replied.

'From up north, eh?' he asked.

'Aye, Yorkshire.'

By now the battle with the unseen fish was reaching the tide's edge and the angler had begun to back up the shingle, pulling the fish into the broken water that broke against the shingle beach. Although all the other rods were taking a keen interest in the proceedings, for reasons I could not understand no one was making any effort to help land the fish.

'Have you got a gaff?' I asked.

'No, it got forgotten in the rush. But don't worry, Ken'll land it!'

'Should I help?' I asked lifting up my gaff for inspection.

'If you do, don't you dare miss it!' came the reply.

It was rude, impertinent and high-handed of me, but what the hell. I turned and walked towards the sea's edge where the fish, a good Cod, was now clearly visible through the breaking wave. I looked at the angler, who now was looking at me and the fish with what appeared to be growing concern.

'Shall I help?' I asked.

'Yes. Yes … but don't miss it!'

I put my hand on the line and walked down into the sea's edge. All the time the fish kept coming in towards me. I lined up the fish and pushed out the gaff until it was under the head of the Cod. A quick lift and it was on. I turned and walked out of the sea with the gaff held high in my right hand. The successful angler muttered something and took the gaff and fish from me, and disappeared up the shingle towards his tackle bag. It was weighed and went 26 lb, a beautiful grey-backed, gold-spotted and white-flanked Cod, the biggest rod and line caught Cod I had ever seen.

'Thank you for that, Yorkie, you did right.'

It weighed 26 lbs . . . The author's Dungeness friend with his spectacular catch

'It was intrusive and rude on my part but it worked, and that was a cracking fish, best I've ever seen caught!'

Within minutes another rod was in and this time it was the angler who had struck up conversation with me. Of course I stayed to watch.

'You going to do the honours, Yorkie? With yer gaff?'

Of course I did, and this Cod a mirror of the first and weighed in at 23 lb. To me, who had undergone four days of not even having a bite, to see two 20-plus pounders landed in the space of 15 minutes was overwhelming, and I said so.

'So, how the hell do you know where to fish?' I asked. 'The water is so deep here you can't tell where there are holes and where there are not.'

'Look, its no secret, not really. We ...'– he looked and waved his arm towards his friends – 'we've been coming to Dunge since we were kids. We had to cycle in them days, now we come by car or even a minibus. So we know by and large just where to come and when.'

'Obviously!' I said. 'And thank you all for your hospitality and allowing me the privilege to land your fish, something never to be forgotten. Thank you'.

I began to walk back along the beach to my friends when the angler who had befriended me called me back.

'Look, Yorkie. You here tomorrow?'

'After seeing what's just happened, most certainly!'

'Well, listen. When we've gone we'll put a marker into the top of the shingle where we think you'll do well tomorrow. We'll not be here tomorrow, see?'

'Wow! Thanks, that's great! Thank you very much. We'll look out for it.'

And the next morning we did, and found it. It was about 60 yards further west than where the six local rods had been yesterday, and there were no other rods in sight save the usual crowd on the Point. It was a cooler morning than yesterday and visibility was poor, with shards of mist over the sea and tight against the shore away to our right.

David Morton with his fish of 13.5 lbs and our new mate with the first of his two fish,
this one just over 19 lbs

We'd been fishing for about half an hour when I had a bite, and after a bit of a scrap a 5 lb Codling identical in colour scheme to those caught yesterday slid up the shingle to me. As this was my first Dungeness Cod I was delighted, and it seemed to jolt my companions for they both decided to rebait and have a new cast.

For Martin, his anxiety to do well and cast a country mile overcame his natural caution and he mistimed the cast absolutely, producing the biggest backlash I have probably ever seen in my life. Martin spent the rest of the day trying his damndest to undo the tangle.

David was more fortunate, and fishing the furthest left of the three of us put away a long clean cast that disappeared into the ever-moving mist that still prevailed. I, too, cast and we settled down to await the results. About ten minutes later David's rod tip dipped and after a bit of a struggle he landed yet another Cod, identical in colouring to the others. We weighed it: it went 13 lb 8 oz. We were euphoric. All the frustrations, the damn battery problem, the weather, all of it aimed at pouring cold water on our efforts, had failed. We had come and had succeeded.

At that moment there appeared over the brow of the top of the shingle bank behind us a solitary figure in jacket and short waders, carrying a bulky rod bag and haversack that dangled from his right arm.

'Good morning, gentlemen,' he said as he walked through the shingle and stopped by Martin, who had returned to his task of trying to untangle his backlash now that the excitement with David's fish had passed.

'Mornin',' we replied.

'Would you chaps mind if I were to fish over there?' He pointed to a spot away to our left. 'I'll not get in your way, I promise!'

'Be our guest, mate,' we all said in chorus. And our 'guest' moved away to our left and began to get himself organised. A few minutes later he had tackled up and walked across to where the three of us were standing.

'OK?' he asked.

'Aye, when you like,' we chorused.

He walked away to our left and turned side on to the sea, swung the lead on a 4-foot drop and turned sharply and cast. The lead went about 60 yards and with that he went back to his rod stand, a pair of bamboos tied with strong cord, laid the rod upon the stand and tightened the slack line. 'That'll do fine,' he said to no one in particular and walked back to his haversack and rodbag.

He looked like a small-town solicitor, with that kind of bearing and a walk that was utterly confident in all he did. His tackle was to all appearances brand new or very rarely used. A Hardy Longbow and an ABU reel, just about the best equipment you could buy at that time, and it seemed somehow quite appropriate for the man. A few minutes later he came down the shingle carrying another rod, this time an 8-foot spinning rod, coupled to a small fixed spool reel more suited to fishing for Roach by a river bank than anything to do with sea fishing, and hanging from the tip was a drop of line and three brass booms, each hook baited with what looked like ragworm. The drop was terminated with an old-fashioned clock lead.

'This,' he said as he walked past us, 'is to catch a sole, for my wife!' And with that he cast the lead and its trace no more than about 40 yards. He then wound in the slack line and then laid the rod alongside his Longbow on the bamboo support. Satisfied that he'd done all that needed to be done he walked over to where the three of us still stood, watching our respective rods.

'Well,' he asked, 'how have you done this morning?'

We told him and he was about to say something when David yelled out that he'd had a bite '... on t' big rod!'

We all turned to look and as we did so the Longbow was pulled down hard by the tip and both rods and the stand fell over. By now our visitor had reached the rods. He picked up the Longbow and lifted the rod tip up; it was immediately jagged down very hard. He was not holding the rod as he should, but was cradling it as he tried to hold the bucking rod and lift the spinning rod, now laid askew on the shingle, back onto the bamboo stand.

144

'Hey up, mate. I'll do that.' And David quickly lifted the smaller rod back onto the bamboo stand.

With that the Longbow went from being cradled to being held with a degree of sense, and he began to reel in while the rod leaned over into a lovely curve of induced pressure and no little weight. I went for our gaff and made my way to the water's edge. It was a good fish and went very well, and was giving the visitor a hard time as he tried to keep the rod up and reel in the line at the same time.

'Back up,' said David. 'Back up and don't give it any slack line!' Our visitor did as he was told and slowly began to walk backwards up the shingle. By now the fish, a great thrashing Cod, was in the small onshore surf and I swung the gaff and lifted the fish high as I turned to walk back up the beach to the waiting rod.

'A very good fish, mate, a cracker!' I said as I handed the gaff handle to the visitor.

'Yes, yes. Thank you!'

It was a bit darker-backed than the fish of the day before, but still had that dark grey back with golden speckled flanks and stark white belly. We weighed it and it went just over 19 lb. Yet again we were speechless.

'Did ya see that? He didn't cast 70 yards! And worra a fish!' said Martin.

'Hey!' I yelled. 'Bring yer fish over 'ere. We want a photo of you and David here with both fish on show.'

He did as I had asked and I took their photo. I had no sooner pressed the shutter than Martin, who had kept his eyes on all the rods, yelled out 'Bite!'

We turned to look, and there on the shingle was the visitor's spinning rod being pulled across the shingle, the bamboo stand sprawled at a crazy angle but still upright.

The visitor ran as fast as he could across the shingle and picked up the butt of the rod, and swept it backwards and upwards in one long arc. The rod suddenly stopped dead as if it had run into a brick wall, and in an instant had curled over into almost a semi-circle.

'Hell!' said David 'its another good un!'

And it was, except this time it took a deal longer than the first Cod. The rod was only a light spinning rod and the reel a freshwater fixed spool reel, so he was unable to exert any kind of real pressure when it was required. But soon it was in the light surf and was gaffed and ashore. If we were speechless at the first fish, this second Cod, identical in every respect to the first, when weighed went 15 lb 8 oz.

'Bloody Norah!' said a much-chastened Martin as he made his way back to his still badly tangled reel. 'Two great fish ... can't cast for tuppence ... and after "soles for t' wife"! Ye gods, I don't believe it.'

Five minutes later our recently arrived visitor had packed up all his tackle, put both fish into a strawbag and was on his way home.

'Many thanks, gentlemen!' he said as he passed by on his way up the beach, back the way he had come barely 40 minutes before. We fished on but had ne'r a touch despite our very best efforts, including Martin clearing his backlash and fishing keenly.

Our holiday did continue, including a trip to Admiralty Pier, but we could not hold bottom, try as we might, and so a very mixed week that began in failure ended in a kind of triumph for the three of us. It had been a huge holiday. We had heard of 10-pounders or more caught in the Filey area, read about fish in the middle teens or even twenties, but all landed a very long way from Filey. But this week we had witnessed first-hand two fish over 20 lb, a rank amateur taking two cracking Cod inside a quarter of an hour (unheard of, let alone witnessed!), and we had had a 13-pounder! We were delighted, chuffed, and the real bonus for us was that we were full of confidence for the future. And so we returned home.

Five of us returned to Dungeness a year later, staying this time in a local single-storey clapboard bungalow. It was, as my diary reports, 'A great holiday ... but the fishing was very poor. A south-east wind on arrival that lasted all week producing gin clear water, slight seas no Codling at all, just Pouting and Whiting.' It had other distractions though: funny, often hilarious moments that even today raise many a laugh, and the hospitality given to us by the locals was exemplary, thoughtful and kind. But there was no successful fishing despite extensive efforts that included a visit to Denge Marsh. But you cannot beat the weather; be it stormy, or as here unseasonally mild, soft winds from the south-east producing conditions that in summertime would have produced Mackerel and float fishing, but were certainly unsuitable for 'Cod bashing'.

One Saturday in late April 1968 I asked around my friends to see if any one of them fancied being my navigator during a investigative trip down the Holderness coastline to see whatever there was in the way of accessible beaches other than Skipsea. I ended up going on my own!

Armed with an OS map of the East Riding I decided to drive south as far as Withernsea, and then return home trying to follow the coastline as closely as was possible. Doing this and driving is never easy, and so it proved, but I had a stroke of luck as I drove south beyond Aldbrough. The road between Aldbrough and Withernsea is as twisty a road as you could find anywhere, and in bad weather, frost, snow or fog, a bit of a nightmare. On this day the conditions were ideal and as I drove on past Grimston I suddenly saw a signpost all but hidden in a roadside hedge which read 'Hilston'. Looking at the map I saw that the road, if followed, led to the sea's very edge, and so it proved. After driving past a well-maintained and large private garden complete with tennis court, on past a terrace of houses, and then a little further on down a dip in the road what looked like a church specially imported from Holland, I came to a T-junction and turned left. As I drove down that arrow-straight road I could see, a good mile ahead of me, the sea: a long grey line edged with blue-black clouds heralding the rain that was to come later in the day.

At the road's end was a right turn and the road then ran south almost parallel with the cliff edge until it reached the village of Tunstall, about half a mile further south. I parked the car by the road side just short of the corner and walked 80 yards across a ploughed field to the cliff edge.

I could hardly believe my eyes. At the foot of some readily accessible cliffs was a steep and very wide sandy beach that stretched several hundred yards south from where I was standing. As the beach made its way north it narrowed but kept its steep profile. So good was this beach that I sat down on the cliff edge and tried to take in what I was looking at and retain it in my mind. Much to my surprise it was evident that it was hardly fished: there were no tell-tale signs of car tyres on the grass verges by the roadside where I had parked, there were no obvious pathways down onto the beach, even though the cliffs offered no difficulty in access whatever. Even if they had been difficult, a rope would have resolved the problem absolutely.

After a while I stood up and walked along the cliff edge, climbing the slight incline up to a spot where once there had been some habitation (we later called this spot 'Bungalows' and it was to be a favoured car parking spot for a number of years). From here I could see for a long way south, and my delight at what I could see just grew.

Having seen all I wanted to, I decided to continue my survey and keep looking, but my heart was just not in it because somehow or other I knew that this beach, at a place we came to call 'Hilston', would serve us well for some time to come; and so it proved. Although a group of us visited Hilston the day after my discovery we did not do well – it was late in the season after all – but then before we knew it winter fishing was upon us.

On the first Saturday of October 1968, Fred, Noddy and myself went to Hilston. It was a mild day, heavily overcast with little to no wind and a big tide; it was the first day of my annual holiday and it was to be a memorable day. On arrival on the cliff top the sight before us was one that I would never, ever see again: 200 yards off the low-water mark were lines of high, breaking waves, 4 feet high, falling onto a high sand bar formed by the famed 'East Coast Drift'. Between this breaking water and the beach was a gulley of (no doubt) deep water – a classic 'lay' (the broken water) situation. Usually such gullies and lays are on the low-water line, rarely visible at sea, and such gullies invariably hold fish.

How this unique situation had occurred could only be attributable in part, as I've said, to the East Coast Drift, the basic north–south current that flows off the Yorkshire coast. Some time during the previous summer this same current had for reasons of its own

148

dumped many tons of sand and gravel brought from further north along this part of the coastline. It had produced a bank of sand 30 yards wide and probably only a couple of feet higher than the surrounding seabed. This lay ran from Grimston a couple of miles north of us as far south as Tunstall, about a mile to our right. This same current had also flushed out the sand between the lay and the shore; this sand had been dumped on the lay as well. Essentially, it was a sandy reef, and the implications of it were such that it could only possibly mean fish, and the hair on the back of my neck bristled … The surf on the beach at the low-water mark was reflective of the waves breaking on the lay: 4 feet high, rising quickly, and crashing down onto a beach that was still as wide and steep as on my first visit. And with not another rod in sight.

My diary for that memorable day states:

it was a big tide of 17 feet with long deep swells pouring out of the east to pound the deeply shelving beach. The fish were well off and casts had to be over 90 yards to pick up fish. Of the 66 lb of Codling we landed, we missed aproximately 50% of the bites we had … and we returned some undersized fish.

Five of us returned the next day, but we were late in arriving and in those days we were not aware of the importance of reading the beach so as to make sure that the spot we fished was more likely to hold fish. My diary states:

We arrived late, unfortunately, to find that the sea had already flooded the beach so we fished what we were sure was the 'hole' we had fished the day before … but the final resultant weights of fish caught indicates that some of us were in the 'hole' sometimes and out of it more than enough … 52 lb of Codling taken.

Nonetheless, eight rods had caught 118 lb of Codling over two tides! In our history of fishing this was brilliant, although the biggest

Codling barely reached 4 lb. We had never taken so much fish over a whole winter when rock fishing, and we left Hilston later that evening looking forward to a great winter's fishing.

In the event we were not disappointed, but it did not turn out as well as that October weekend had promised. The total catch taken between 5th October 1968 and 30th March 1969 was 892 lb, with three notable fish:

Martin Scotter's Cod of exactly 15 lb. Taken at Skipsea on 22nd December 1968.
Noddy Bannister's Thornback Skate of 13 lb 5oz. Taken at Skipsea on 13th October 1968.
Norman Viles's Thornback Skate of 12 lb 8 oz. Taken at Skipsea (the Tank Blocks at Road's End) on 20th October 1968.

There were many things memorable about Martin's excellent Cod that are worthy of report. My diary reported:

A bright but windy day, with a great tide … we found a nearly circular and deep hole about 9 yards in diameter, on past the Tank Blocks on the low-water mark. What had caused such an anomaly we could not even begin to guess … we fished it from 3.30 p.m. until 6.40 p.m. And in that time the wind radically increased and it began to rain. The wind was due south and about force 6 gusting force 8 produced a large onshore surf. Then, just on dusk Noddy had three Codling in three casts all just over 3 lb apiece which was followed by Martin's rod having a cracking bite. There then followed a good surging scrap and then in the white scouring surf a large dorsal, then rear dorsal appeared with large attendant tail … Fantastic! I gaffed it first time and it was immediately weighed – 15 lb exactly! The fish was caught two hours before high water, taken on lug-worm, cast into the very centre of the circular hole, some 40 yards out.

We were euphoric! It was one of the best fish taken over that winter and although it fell to Martin's rod it was the result of all our efforts that had begun during the summer of 1963, five and a half years before.

In retrospect I now agree with Fred, who at the time said that the last thing we should have done that night was to pack up and adjourn to the Board Inn to celebrate. He argued, rightly I believe now, that Martin's fish would not have been on its own, and that hole had already produced three Codling prior to Martin's fish, so it stood to sense that there would be more. 'And when did you last see a hole like that one, eh? A one-off and it was ours and we left it. Crackers!' We'll never know now.

Winter fishing from October 25th 1969 to 22nd March 1970 was again a very mixed bag, and the total weight caught by five rods – John Addis, Fred Hall, Dave Morton, Martin Scotter and myself – was 226 lb. This was an enormous drop in weight from the previous year, 666 lb. This can be explained in some ways by the fact that Martin and David rarely went, and there were many days of very few fish and a great many small Codling that all went back.

For once I took the best fish of the season, a fish of 10 lb exactly, followed on the next cast by a fish of 9 lb exactly. Fred took a Spur Dog of 6 lb which made quite a change for the Yorkshire coast, although it is not recorded in any of my diaries.

But this winter had a very memorable February. In fact I would go so far as to say that it was the most memorable February for a great many years for Filey's sea fishing. It began with John Jenkinson ('Bonzo Junior') taking a Cod from Ling Rock of just over 29 lb, which was pretty amazing for Filey Brigg, only for this to be almost equalled in weight by Frank Colling's Cod of 28½ lb. What made Frank's even more amazing was that it was taken from Ben Storey's Nab (Black Hole Top) during an FBAS match, at night, and that the landing of the fish involved Frank climbing halfway down the Nab to get the fish up. The mind boggles!

151

Fish of a Lifetime

Then the cherry on the cake so to speak. On Sunday 8th February 1970, Bob Yarker caught his fish of a lifetime. Bob Yarker had told me sometime in the mid-1960s that Filey Brigg End on a big tide in mid-January was a very special place for a big fish. I cannot tell you that he fished Brigg End during this period every year, but knowing Bob, he very probably did. And there had to be something about the tides and weather that made this venue special to Bob on this particular Sunday, even though it was a fortnight after his favourite time. As far as I am aware he fished it alone, and that proved to be signicant.

Nor am I aware as to what bait he used, but you can perm any one from lugworm, crab or mussels. Maybe he used a cocktail of baits. He certainly used his trusty Greenheart rod and Scarborough reel. He must have begun fishing at the 1.30 p.m. start time for the Scarbough Rock Anglers weekly match. It is a fair guess that he got down as far as Yacht Cills, the very furthest an angler or anyone can get at Brigg End, for this particular Sunday had the second-biggest tide of the year. His cast would have been a typical Yarker cast of quality: long and straight, probably 70 or 80 yards; it is unlikely it went any further, casting out at an angle of 45 degrees from the line of the Brig, more than likely on slack water or on the very first of the flood.

I do not know what happened as to bite or struggle but it must have to have been extremely hard and fraught. I do know that he landed this huge Cod at Brigg End, a kelp-infested jungle of weed, of rock and hard scar edges. To have lifted that fish from the water, even if only to swim it into the wash of Brigg End, was no mean feat. What Bob did on that Sunday, on his own, should go down in local angling history as absolutely amazing, and be commemorated in a very special way. It weighed, some three hours after landing and a difficult journey to those scales, a massive 33 lb 7½ oz.

Bob told me some time later that after he had it ashore he realised that he had given his all in landing it. He was spent, undone, knackered. He sat on the Step (a geological fault that crosses the Brigg, 100 yards east of High Brigg, running north to south ending up in Crab Hole) desperate to get back his breath and strength. Meanwhile, the tide was making fast and he had to get out and off the Brigg as quickly as he could, but as he thought about the walk that faced him to Carr Naze, the climb up Carr Naze and then the even longer walk to his parked motorcycle on Country Park, he felt utterly incapable. But he did it, and his magnificent fish is still both a club and county record to this day.

Bob was a very good angler, a thinking man's angler, a private man, and one who it was a privilege to know. I admired him a great deal. His early death in 1976, aged only 55, was a sad loss to angling in general and an even greater loss to sea angling in Scarborough especially. Just what effect the depth of effort he made to land that fish had upon his health, only Bob would have known, but I am sure it had some significance.

During that same week I too experienced the thrill of a 'big fish'. As previously described I went back to Ireland in October 1970, and during that holiday I caught a memorable Bass of 9 ½ lb that had a profound affect upon my angling. I had no inclination to go fishing at all upon my return to England, so since I was not present when our group went fishing, no records of catches were made between October 1970 and April 1971. That winter will be remembered as the winter of chat Codling, literally thousands of them invading the beaches with a fierce enthusiasm and taking all the bait meant for their bigger brothers.

Then, in that memorable February week in 1969, I too had a very brief but unforgettable moment…

Good Night, Bad Night

It was very dark; hardly a star was visible through the thin cloud that completely hid the pale crescent of the new moon. There was little wind and it was cold, as one would expect in mid-January. A match flared into bright yellow light, illuminating Fred's bearded features and the dimness of the van's interior, and was applied to the wire-clad wick beneath the glass shield of the Tilley lamp. The meths caught at once and a blue flame ran quickly around the wick and began to rise up and over the white-dusted mantle that sat above it.

'You'd better shut yon door, Noddy,' said Fred, moving the lamp farther into the darker recesses of the van, 'there's over-much draught in here to get t' lamp a going.'

Noddy dutifully shut the doors, only pausing to look at his watch in the flickering light.

'What time is it, Noddy?' I asked.

'Half past eleven.'

'We must be daft, absolutely crackers, all three of us to be here at dead o' night to dig bloody bait,' I said.

'We'd no choice, 'ad we, with all of us working and not being able to dig bait tomorrow noon as we'd hoped,' answered Noddy, handing me my fork from the cluster of forks and buckets that leaned against the van's side.

It was true, of course; none of us was able to dig the noon tide the next day so we had no choice but to dig bait at midnight if we were to fish the next night and its big tide.

By now the inside of the van was white with light and Noddy opened the rear doors to reveal Fred, his back against the van side, pumping the lamp hard. The Tilley was duly passed to Noddy who stood it on the cobbled slipway.

'C'mon, we'd better make a start,' I said, 'it's almost low water already.'

'Aye, tha's right; you bring t' Tilley, Noddy, we'll not need three forks, just the one.'

Before Noddy had chance to reply Fred was off, and fast disappearing into the dark towards the distant sound of heavy surf. I picked up the bucket and set off after him, with Noddy bringing the lamp behind me. We walked in silence across the dark, deserted beach, the only sounds that of the sea and the hissing Tilley, its light sweeping the dark sand as it swung gently from Noddy's hand.

Unexpectedly we came upon a great horde of gulls standing stark and white against the blackness of the night. The gulls, using the beach as their overnight roost, suddenly took fright and rose with one accord, the beating of their wings and discordant cries rending the cold night air and awaking their more somnolent companions.

The ebb was enormous and it seemed a long time before we reached the sea's edge and that band of sand where we were to dig the big black lugworm. Fred, leaning on his fork, the soft red glow of his cigarette hanging low from his left hand, was clearly silhouetted against the lines of white surf that rose, curled and fell with a continuous roar behind him. At the sea's edge the wet sand was touched with the bright spots of phosphorescence that momentarily danced in each dying run of surf. Fred, heedless of the cold beauty of the sea and the night, was as ever eager to get on with the job in hand.

'Bring yon light, Noddy. Thar's a good patch o' casts 'ere.'

Noddy obediently brought over the lamp and as the light swept across the quickly drying sand, everywhere we could see the large cartwheel casts of the lugworm.

''Ell, there's a ton of 'em, an' good uns an' all,' said Noddy.

'Aye, but you stop swinging that flamin' lamp and hold it steady. Right, here goes.'

So saying, Fred put his fork 12 inches in front of a large circular

156

worm cast that had traces of coal dust in it, and began to cut through the hard-packed sand with the ease that is only born of years of practice. Quickly, simply, the depth of the hole he had dug increased, a clean-cut trench that moved from sea to cast with a prompt rhythm that was admirable.

'There's 'is 'ole,' said Noddy, although such a comment was utterly unnecessary.

'Aye, I see it,' grunted Fred, his breath coming in short sharp bursts that formed little clouds that hung suspended before him for a short time before they drifted away into the night. The hole lit by the lamp was deep now, taking Fred four full spit lengths to reach bottom.

'This time, Fred,' I said.

'Aye,' was his short reply.

Fred brought the fork right down to the bottom of the trench, and with one great heave lifted out a spit of sand and dumped it on the beach; there from the sand protruded the dull yellow tail of a worm.

'Good un,' said Noddy as he carefully put the big black lugworm in the bucket. It was a good worm, all of 9 inches long and of a kind noted for toughness to withstand the cast and to fish well.

Fred had moved on to a fresh cast and soon he had another worm to join the first, but this time it was bigger by a good 2 inches.

'Give us that fork,' said Noddy, 'and give us a go.'

Fred handed Noddy the fork and he, too, began to follow the same pattern that Fred had set, and so it continued for the next hour, with each of us in turn doing our share of digging. Sometimes we had more than the one worm from a hole and twice we had the unexpected bonus of a large ragworm. It was a little after ten to one in the morning when we thought we had enough and called a halt. By now the thin crescent of the new moon had come through the overcast cloud and the tide, now flooding hard, had begun to overrun the holes we had dug earlier.

''Ells bells, I'm knackered,' wheezed Fred as he struggled to stand upright. 'I could kill a fag.'

'Here, have one of mine,' I said.

'What time tomorrow night, Nav?' asked Noddy, who seemed unbent by his efforts.

'You be at Fred's at half past six, I'll see you there. That all right by you, Fred?'

'Aye, ah'll be there.'

We came off the beach in silence; it was 1.15 and the car was covered with a mantle of frost.

The night was cold and very black. Overhead the plush velvet of darkness was scattered with an infinity of bright stars. Two Tilley lamps, placed to give maximum illumination to our activities, hissed and sighed in an almost perfect unison of sound. There was no wind; the only sound was that of the lamps and the deep heavy swell that lifted, probed and growled around the cliff foot 40 feet below us.

Ben Storey's Nab, for that is the name given to the place from which we were fishing, is an uneven and rugged platform of boulder clay supported on a sheer cliff of sandstone that stands some 90 feet high above and behind us. A steep and narrow path leads up from the platform to the cliff top high above it, and the cliffs themselves go on to form the promontory that is the start of the famous Filey Brigg. At the cliff foot, permanently deep water hides in its dark depths an area of very heavy ground; a tangle of boulders both large and small, separated by areas of a living jungle of kelp and patches of sand, ground that by its very nature is a perfect haven to support and protect the marine life that forms part of the food chain; a living larder for fish of prey.

'It looks good, Nav,' said Fred, carefully threading a large black lugworm onto a newly sharpened 6/0. He straightened up, looking out into the dark of the night, and sniffed. 'Ah can smell 'em. They're there, right enough.'

So saying, he picked up his rod and, holding the trace carefully in his left hand, walked past me towards the cliff edge on my right.

'I hope that ain't wishful thinking, Fred,' said Noddy, who was still busy preparing his gear.

'Nay, Noddy, think on: a big tide, a falling-off sea, still lumpy, and a night as cold as this … there'll be fish ternight.'

Fred turned his back to the sea, letting the trace fall from his hand, and it fell away from him in a long arc, and having reached the end of its swing began to return towards him. He dropped the rod tip and the lead began to swing away from him again, but much quicker now; with Fred pulling the rod round hard and turning into the cast, the rod compressed into a deep curve. He hit it hard and then the rod unwound: the lead had gone, only the rod tip pointing to its trajectory.

Noddy followed him, then I, too, had cast and the rods were laid down on the cliff top, their tips projecting over the edge, each multiplier out of gear, ratchets on. We had each cast to different positions: Noddy well to our left, Fred almost straight off, while my bait also lay to our left, between Fred's and Noddy's. Now we had to wait.

We did not talk; each was utterly immersed in his own thoughts and dreams. The cold was oppressive and clinging, no matter what one did to ease it. Out in the darkness blinked the odd light of the local keelboats, ever trawling the same run of ground, scarping away the sand to leave barren rock. Far to our left, the lights of Scarborough twinkled through the night air, belying the distance that separated us from its busy streets and alleyways. It was a night of quiet stillness.

Suddenly, Fred stood up and flicked his cigarette out into the void, looking keenly at his rod: I too looked, but like mine, it was unmoving. Fred's gaze remained on his rod.

'What's up, Fred?' said Noddy.

Fred did not answer, but continued to watch. Then, just as my eyes were about to go back to my rod I saw it. The tip of the ABU dipped very slightly and came back to its original position.

'There's summat at it, Fred,' I said.

Fred still did not reply but continued his vigil. The rod tip dipped again but this time with greater vigour and remained down, the ratchet screaming loudly. Fred was on his feet, hand to rod, the reel put into gear, the ratchet off, all in one smooth movement. Standing in a partially crouched stance, the rod held out in front of him, Fred was like a coiled spring, tense and waiting. At the instant of the bite Fred swept the rod back in a long, high lift, then it literally stopped dead, as though it had hit a wall.

''Ell fire, I 'it 'im!' said Fred, moving back a pace from the cliff edge.

'Looks good, Fred,' said Noddy.

'He is … a good un,' answered Fred in gasps, reeling hard, the rod held high on his chest, the rod tip dancing to the continual boring of the fish. Fred must have got it coming 20 yards when he stopped reeling, the rod held hard over in a tight circle.

'He's fast, dammit,' said Fred.

He dropped the rod and put the reel out of gear, pulling line off the spool and feeding it through the rings. He waited, watching the loose line fall away from the rod tip and disappear down into the black gulf.

The minutes passed slowly. I looked up and saw high above me a fine bright spot of light moving across the sky; a man-made star of light – a good omen, I hoped. I looked at Fred again but he was still unmoving.

'Try it now, Fred,' said Noddy, unable to control his impatience.

A moment passed, then the rod was pulled down hard, viciously, and Fred, realising that the fish had swum clear of the trouble and was trying again to reach the deeper offshore water, and that he had it in the open, began to pick up the loose line. Reeling hard, the rod held high, Fred kept the pressure on and this time it worked, for the fish was slowly coming. Noddy and I moved to the cliff edge and we began to sweep the water with our headlights; both lights came together at the same place, on a moving roll of heavy swell almost directly below us. There, in the spot of light, was a splash of water, the white flank of a fish.

'It's a good fish, Fred, certainly in double figures,' I said.

I went closer to the cliff edge, looking for the way down to the small, narrow landing that time, the elements and the sea itself had carved from the rock. If I could get down, there might be a slim chance of reaching the fish.

'You see it, Nav?' asked Fred.

'Aye, it's straight below us. I was thinking of lifting it up onto the ledge.'

'You'll never do it, it's too big. I've got a better idea,' replied Fred. 'You, Norman, stand on yon point of rock, as far to our right as you can get, OK?'

'Yes, but what do you have in mind?'

'Standing on that point of rock, you hold my line, giving that fish whatever line it wants, but no slack; I'll go back up to the cliff top with the rod, letting out line as I go …'.

The idea was good. Once on the cliff top, Fred could walk along the edge for 50 yards to another path leading down to the next nab along the coastline. At the bottom of this track an iron ladder was fixed to sheer rock face, giving access to the rocks below. Once down the ladder, Fred would reel in all the line he could until it was taut between us, then signal with his lamp, and I would free the line and Fred would reel like a madman, hoping to pick up all the slack and bring the fish over from below our vantage point to the rock edge at his feet. There he would have the chance to lift it, with the help of the swell, over the scar's edge and onto the flat run of rock that was a few feet below him. A scramble down onto this flat rock and, he hoped, the fish would be his. A wild, outrageous idea that had every chance of working. Fred pushed the rod tip at me and I took hold of the 28 lb test nylon line and began to wait for Fred, who was already on his way up to the cliff top, letting out line as he went. Having reached there, he paused to check that it had not fouled on anything in his mad dash up the steep clay path. I felt him pull hard, twice; so far so good, it had cleared any obstacles and we were in with a chance.

'Noddy, quick, pour some coffee from the flask onto the clay and make a small mud ball … hurry.'

Noddy, looking at me as though I was some kind of fool, did as I asked. I looked up to see that Fred had reached the path that led down to the next nab on from ourselves. Again, I felt him pull the line hard, and as I looked out across the void to where he was almost running down the cliff path, my headlight caught the fine thin vein of line glinting faintly. From its direction I could tell that it was still free; it looked like the gods were with us. Once Fred was on the ladder, the chances of his line fouling were slight, but you could never tell.

My mind quickly returned to the problem in hand when a sudden surge of the fish far below me dragged the line from between my fingers, but it was a tired effort and after it gained a few yards, I retrieved the lost line. Relieved that the fish was too tired to cause concern, I looked down again to my right and saw that Fred was now on the ladder, and it appeared that the line still had not fouled on anything.

'Here, Nav, here's that ball of mud you wanted.' Noddy was handing me a small ball of rich red boulder clay. 'What on earth do you want it for?' he asked.

'To help throw the line clear of the cliff face, otherwise it might catch and Fred will lose his fish.'

'I hope it works. It sounds a wild idea though. What happens when it reaches Fred's end ring?'

'I don't think it will survive the drop or the sea.'

Suddenly, from my right, came the flash of Fred's lamp. He had reached the bottom of the iron ladder and no doubt was waiting nervously for my signal. Now we would see if the idea was going to work. I flashed my lamp at him, heard the faint sound of his voice, and sent the small clay pebble flying out into the void.

'It's no good, Nav, we must have a better way of getting a good fish up 'ere than this,' Noddy said.

It was true, of course, but the prospect of a fish as big as this had never occurred to us as being a problem we would have to face.

'Aye, Noddy, I realise that. But this is one hell of a time to mention it.'

We'd soon know, though, for Fred should have picked up all the slack line by now. Even as I thought it, I saw the flash of his light on the water at his feet. As the light moved erratically over the water below Fred, we saw that the flat area of scar beneath him was awash as a sudden lift of swell poured across it. The light moved around all over the surface of the water, then settled in one spot.

'He's got it up!' cried Noddy.

Even as we watched, we saw the scar bare, the water running quickly off it; then by the action of Fred's headlight he must have gone down onto the scar. Suddenly from far below us came a distant cry.

'He must have got it,' said Noddy hopefully.

Fred's light was now going upwards. He must be on his way back and we'd soon know if the idea had worked.

It seemed an age before the light from Fred's headlamp began to come down the path that led from the cliff top to our platform. Noddy, unable to control his excitement, had run halfway back up the path to meet Fred. Then, the lights were doused and from out of the blackness came Fred, smiling hugely, his rod held in his left hand, while hanging from his right was a great flank of white: a Cod, and a very good one, too.

I pushed the hook of the scales through the large gill case and by the light of the Tilley looked eagerly at the wavering pointer. It settled on 11½ lb.

'First thing in the morning, Nav,' said Fred, taking a cigarette from a battered packet, 'we are going to have a dropnet made. I don't think I could go through that again.'

Neither could I, but by hell it had been worth it. Fred went to his gear, put the Cod down and stood for a moment, admiring it in the soft light of the Tilley. It was a beautiful fish: grey-backed, white-bellied, with dappled white and grey flanks flecked with gold – a true 'off' fish.

At this instant my rod tip nodded slightly, hardly visible. Noddy's voice came to me from the shadows to my left.

'Norman! Bite!'

'I see it. Don't fret.'

I picked up my rod, dropping the tip so that it pointed to where I hoped a Cod was mouthing that big black bunch of lugworm. I stood

163

for what seemed an age, my whole body tense, my heart thumping as it does when I am about to strike a fish.

Then the rod tip was pulled down strongly. I held tight onto the large handle of my ABU 9000, and struck as hard as I was able. As the rod came back towards my shoulder it stopped absolutely dead, as though a great hand had grabbed hold of it. Then, almost immediately, the fish far below began to go mad. The rod was pulled down violently, line going taut between the fingers of my left hand where I held it tight against the rod. I had to ease off the star drag and the spool spun into life, line streaming out, the rod being shaken with real force as the fish shook its head and moved irresistibly towards the deep water to my left.

'By 'ell, looks like it is another good fish,' said Noddy.

'It is. It is one 'ell of a fish … couldn't stop it. 'Ell it's off again!'

It was charging its way to my left with such power that the spinning spool began to burn my finger that I had laid against it.

''Ellfire, he's a good un. Believe me, a real beauty. If only I can stop his rushes.'

'Don't talk, you twit, concentrate,' said Fred urgently.

The fish eventually stopped, and I began to think it had gone to ground in the heavy kelp. I eased the pressure on the rod, and I felt it move, not far but a definite movement. Pushing the reel out of gear I peeled line from the spool and played it down the rings, making sure that the line remained reasonably tight all the time. The next movement was a deal longer than before, and sensing that this was a good time to try and get the fish to come, I dropped the rod tip even farther, then began to reel and pump as though my life depended on it. The rod began to keel over, forming a deep semicircle as the line tightened to the weight of the fish. This fish was heavier than anything I had ever been involved with, and I had made little impression in the course of the battle. After what seemed an age I began to make headway; slowly, with each pump of the rod and turn of the handle, I was beginning to gain ground.

'Keep 'is 'ead up, Norman, for Pete's sake!' yelled a voice, its inherent excitement concealing its owner.

'I'm trying, damn it. I'm trying.'

The battle was beginning to tell on me now, though I had got the fish well towards the base of the cliff, and he was coming a lot easier than before.

'Steady now, Nav,' said Fred, 'move back a bit so that we can get at your line.'

I did as he had said and I could see now that Fred and Noddy both had their headlights shining down onto the heaving broken water at our feet.

'Can't see owt yet,' said Noddy.

'Yes! There he is, there!' screamed Fred, pointing at a spot directly below him and invisible to me.

'For crying out loud, it's bloody enormous! Look at that fish! Just look at the bloody size of it, it's ginormous!' shouted Noddy, almost deafening me.

'A great, big "off" fish. 'Ell it's a great fish,' added Fred, now beginning to reach out to my rod tip with his right hand.

'I'd reckon it's all of twenty pounds. 'Ell, could be a lot more,' said Noddy very quietly.

'Aye, Norman, I'd reckon on it going a good twenty-five pounds,' said Fred in a strictly matter-of-fact voice.

As I had still not seen the fish because of my position 2 yards back from the cliff edge, my emotions upon hearing these varying estimates of the weight of the fish were, to say the very least, alarming because I had yet to get the fish up that towering cliff face.

'Steady, Nav, there's a lot of lift and he's getting very close to the cliff.'

I moved forward a yard.

'Steady, give us a bit of line,' said Fred as his hand took a grip upon the rod tip.

'Are you going to do what Fred did to get 'im up?' asked Noddy.

'I've no choice. I can't possibly lift it, no chance.'

It was at that moment that the wave hit the cliff. I did not see it, I only heard the roar, then the dull thud and I felt the whole cliff shake.

'Ye gods!' said Fred. 'Where the 'ell did that come from?'

165

The rod came light, and I sensed the fish being lifted up. I began to reel instinctively.

'Don't!' screamed Fred.

It was too late. I had reeled in about a couple of feet of line, when the rod tip was pulled down hard. I relaxed my thumb on the spool to enable the fish to take the line just retrieved, but I was not quick enough. There was a sudden lurch of the rod tip; then Fred screamed that there was another wave. It hit the cliff, there was another roar and the whole cliff shook; then I felt the line go slack. I knew it had gone. I just stood stunned, looking at the heaving turmoil of the effect of the two waves far below me, lit by our lamps.

'Rotten 'ell fire,' said Fred.

'Hard luck, Norman,' said Noddy very quietly.

'It must only 'ave bin lip 'ung,' added Fred.

I did not speak. There was nothing I could say.

'Well, Norman, tha' can allus say tha's 'ad one of 'em on t' hook, which is more than a lot of anglers around 'ere can say.'

At least in that there was some consolation.

The Gulley, and Winter 1971/72

As the months passed I found my love of angling grow back from its period of satisfied leisure to its old state of anticipation. It was on a Tuesday, 6th July 1971, a grey, cool evening, when I made my way onto the Brigg alone to try my hand. It took me an hour to find some soft crabs, finding just half a dozen good ones. I began by fishing Ling Rock; the wind was fretful, westerly about force 4, with an occasional shower of rain adding to the scene. The sea was gin clear, with a slight swell.

I began to fish at 6 p.m. and by 7.15 p.m., still on my own, I had not had a bite. I was using my new ABU 464 for the very first time ever for fishing (I had been practicing with it for some weeks) and though my first cast was awful the rest were by far the furthest I'd ever thrown a soft crab in my life. With Ling Rock proving a waste of time and bait I moved down the top end of Gulley Wash to try and fish the bottom of Binks, a very ambitious idea which I would never have considered possible using my Longbow. By casting a 'softie' over 90 yards (quite a feat) I dropped my bait right into the middle of *the* hole.

After about a quarter of an hour, my rod, which was laid on the scar's edge with its tip projecting out over the water below, suddenly had a slight tap. The tip quickly pulled round, then springing back to its original position, the line released, hanging now below the rod tip. Almost immediately the tip and then the rod was pulled violently around. I picked it up. A heavy downward yank. Bang! I was in.

After a great scrap which left my arms aching, up through the dark green water came a deep white-flanked and golden-brown-backed and speckled Cod that took my breath away. In order to land it I had to walk the fish along the scar's edge until I reached a point where the sea was slipping and sliding its way into the Gulley itself and here I was able to swill it into the shallow water of the Gulley's edge. I weighed the fish and it went 10 lb 2 oz, my second-best fish from the Brigg.

Five weeks later I got married to Julie, and my life was to change again. We delayed our honeymoon and went to Ireland in early September. For the second week we went to Waterville, County Kerry, and somehow I found time for some fishing. Waterville had been the base for the previous year's fishing holiday and we visited most of the venues I had fished that year. Whatever was to happen to my fishing life? As we returned home I could only hope that things would not change that much.

Winter fishing began on 25th September 1971 and finished on 19th March 1972. What made this season somewhat different was that it included trips to Cornelian Bay, Castey runlings, Silwicks Bay and Flamborough as well as Bridlington Pier, and that there were seven of us involved in one way or another.

Gross weight caught: 562 lb.
John Addis: 126 lb; best day 7/11/71 = 35 lb; best fish 5 lb.
Fred Hall: 161 lb: Best Day 7/11/71 = 25 lb; best fish 7 lb taken at Cornelian Bay, Scarborough.
Noddy Bannister: 29 lb; Best Day 31/12/71 = 11 lb; best fish 5 lb.
Dave Morton: 41 lb ; Best day 17/3/72 = 22 lb; best fish two of 7 lb each.
Norman Viles: 182 lb: Best Day 16/2/72 = 18 lb; best fish 6 lb.
Most memorable fish: Bass, 2 lb, taken by Norman Viles at Silwicks Bay.

Looking at my diary for this season's fishing I see two comments that are as worthy of note today as they were then. The first concerns keeping of lugworms. Most anglers in those days 'gutted' their worms immediately after digging and froze the results; we never did and always tried to keep them alive as long as was possible. My diary for 22nd February 1972, says:

> The most important discovery of our winter was made today. On Saturday 19th February we had dug some magnificent lugworm. I had put some deep-water seaweed – a bit like bladder wrack save no bladders and coloured cream/fawn – in layers in two plastic buckets with three to four lugworm between each layer. On the Tuesday night at 11 p.m. that bait was still alive, damp (just) and as perfect as one could ever wish, 84 hours after being dug – no fridges, just a cool place and deep-water seaweed.

The second comment was made in January 1972 and concerned the ABU rods, the 484 and 464:

> Once you have mastered these rods (much easier said than done and practice being the key) there really is no other casting rod, and it fishes well too. The distances Fred and I cast out large mussel baits were prodigious and really had to be seen to be believed. It is a hard taskmaster but it is worth the effort.

Today any prospective buyer of a rod for sea fishing has a choice that is mind-boggling. I would say to anyone puzzled as to what to buy that they should try and get hold of an old ABU 464/484. They are heavier than a number of contemporary rods and at 11 feet 6 inches long are not the current concept of what a casting rod should be, but believe me, if you find one, grab it and give it a real go. A friend of mine bought a 484 at a car boot sale in 2012 for £10 and it was in mint nick. The crunch point about rods is this: you need to be able to cast a bait of whatever size, aerodynamic or not, in a straight line, and to do so whatever the weather, night or day, and with no danger to your angling neighbour. Distance comes with practice, but it is not always necessary to be able to cast a country mile, only to be able to put your bait where you want it.

There was one other event that winter that even today defies belief, but what follows is true. The biggest tide of the year occurred on 17th March 1972, and after digging bait at Fraisthorpe, David Morton and I went to Hilston. Hilston was invisible. Thick clammy fog pervaded everything and visibility was no more than a few yards at times as the fog came and went, and it never let up even for a moment. It was so cold and searching that it produced large white droplets on my beard and in my hair, that froze. Sound, too, was exaggerated: you could hear the sound of traffic, no doubt hundreds of yards away, but which sounded as though it were coming on the beach at you.

Then out of the fog came the sound of an engine.

'Bloke on a motor bike,' said David.

'No, that's no motor bike, it's an outboard if it's anything,' I replied.

'An outboard? You nuts, Nav? In this lot? Man, you can't see your hand in front of your face. An outboard? My eye!'

As David said that, I was just about to cast. The noise was still there, that 'Putt! Putt! Putt!' An outboard engine, surely. I swung into my cast and let it go.

As I tried to follow the lead, out of the wall of fog to our left came a small dory, and as my line fell onto the sea the dory went straight across it and cut it as as cleanly as if by a razor. I shouted out as loudly as I could, using pretty strong language which expressed my anger pretty well.

The reaction from the dory as it disappeared into the wall of fog to our right was a mixture of shouts, and the outboard engine quickened its roar. In a moment or two the dory had landed 100 yards along the beach to our right, and my immediate thought was that the helmsman was coming to apologise. He ran along the beach and approached us.

'Where am I?' he asked quite aggressively.

'You gotta be kidding me!' said David.

'No. Where am I?' he asked again.

'You are on the Holderness coast,' I said.

'Holderness? We have been at sea for five hours and utterly lost!'

'Five hours? Have you no compass?'

He ignored my question, and then asked a question which stunned us into a silence of disbelief.

'So, where exactly?' Now there was no mistaking the anger in his voice.

'Hilston,' I replied.

'Hilston?' he said. 'Where the 'ell is that?'

'Three, four miles north of Withernsea.' I said.

'Which is north, then?' Turning round to look towards the cliffs behind us.

'Dear God, man! If this is Holderness, then that,' said David, pointing his arm to his left, 'is north!'

'And Withernsea is where?'

'As I just said. About three or four miles south of here!' I replied.

'Thanks!'

With that he was off, running back into the fog, and within seconds the sound of the outboard motor was heard heading off to sea. David and I just looked at each other. Words failed us both even then, and it still does today, 40-plus years on.

It takes some believing. A 10-foot dory with a Seagull outboard at sea with three grown men aboard on an icy-bound March morning, with fog and visibility down to 15 yards at the very best. For the dory occupants it was a blessing that there was no sea of size running, otherwise their landing would most probably would have been disastrous. Even so! Just what were they doing at sea in such a craft, which was designed for a single person to fish for Cod on the Grand Banks, and there were three of them? No doubt they were up to no good. Drugs? Illegal immigrants? And no compass! Well, we will never know now, will we. An amazing event. The things people will do for money ...

Despite being newly married, and now with a dog to add to my domesticity, I continued my fishing, but not every weekend and rarely on a weekday. However, despite the loss of Martin who had by now moved to Cornwall, and David now off to New Zealand, my fishing mates were as before Fred Hall and Noddy Bannister. The winter fishing of 1972/73 was a better year than the previous one; the three of us, fishing from 7th October 1972 up to 18th February 1973 took 339 lb of fish. For me it was a much curtailed season with marital duties encroaching, especially in the early months of 1973:

Fred: 137 lb; best day: 20/11/72 = 44 lb; best fish = 6 lb Bass.
Noddy Bannister: 54 lb; best day: 5/1/73 = 11lb; best fish = 8 lb Spur Dogfish.
Norman Viles: 148 lb; best day: 20/11/72 = 43 lb; best fish = 14 lb Cod (High Brigg).

It must also be pointed out that Fred had another 'good day'. On 2nd December 1972 he took 29 lb, made up of eight Codling, two of 6 lb and six about 3 lb in weight.

Mention too must be made of that memorable day at Hilston on 20th November 1972 where Fred and I took 22 Codlings between us, best fish a 'Spragg' (Codling) of 7 lb to me, and several fish of 6 lb to both Fred and myself. The total weight landed that day was 87 lb; in the event, we ran out of bait, otherwise we would surely have broken the 100 lb barrier.

We also got around a deal more than in previous years, fishing Bridlington Pier, Cloughton Wyke, Castey, Cornelian Bay and NALGO beach (between Cornelian and Cayton Bay), which added no little variety to our enjoyment.

Of Dominoes And Codling

'It's your drop, Fred,' said Alan as he picked up his pint of bitter.

'Aye, I know,' replied Fred as he looked at the newly laid double six with a look that could only be described as contemptuous.

'Who the 'ell put yon six on t' other end?' Fred asked.

'I did,' answered Colin, 'tha' mind in't on game, Fred lad, is it?'

'C'mon Fred, put down that last six o' thine,' said Alan, a thin line of white froth adorning his top lip.

''Ow the 'ell dus tha' know ah'd a six left?' asked Fred, quickly putting his dominoes up to his chest.

'Cos I'm concentrating, that's why,' replied Alan testily.

Meekly Fred put down a six and four.

'Tha's a lucky so an' so Fred, tha' really is,' said Colin as he laid down a four and three, leaving the six still bare at the other end.

'Dammit, Fred, now I'm knocking!' I said as I vainly looked at the dominoes in front of me for a three or a six that just was not there.

'An' your mind i'nt on t' game either, is it, Norman?' said Alan with a note of triumph in his voice as he laid down the six and three that gave him the game.

It was not, I thought ruefully. That bright November morning we had left home with very high hopes for yet another killing among the Holderness Cod. We had had two days of the finest Cod fishing ever, taking over 150 lb of prime-quality fish in two sessions. All the fish had been between 4 lb and 7 lb, grey-backed and white-bellied with pale golden flanks, Cod that had moved inside from the deeper offshore waters to search and feed from the bountiful larder that is Bridlington Bay. It had not been easy fishing, far from it, for a

173

combination of the autumn spring tides and persistent easterly winds had produced a very big run of surf and tidal bore that necessitated the best of our efforts all the time to succeed.

But now it seemed that the best chance we had ever had to get that 'big un' was slipping from us. Almost as we got out of the car to start the long walk to the bait beds, the wind had veered from east to northerly, and increased in strength from force three to almost gale force. We had driven to our favourite hotspot, knowing that with each hour that passed the wind would be pushing that already difficult surf into a driving onshore run of sea that would make fishing impossible.

And so it proved, for even as we stopped the car we knew our journey had been a fruitless one: the wind, now well above gale force, buffeted and rocked the car with a cold malevolence. Reluctantly, we left the warmth of the car and walked across the short-stubbled fields of long-gathered barley, our heads down to avoid the driving wind that was now spiced with the odd flurry of sleet. At the cliff top, we stood and looked at a view that was awe-inspiring. For as far as the eye could see, the grey, leaden sea was being lifted and torn by the clawing fingers of the gale. It was only two hours after low water, but already the steeply shelving beach was awash with long reaches of spume-topped water, driven far beyond the tideline by waves that rose, curled and fell with a savage intensity. There was nothing to say; we just stood and watched until the wind and the cold became too much and we returned to the car, and so subsequently the Board and the dominoes.

'Well, Norm,' said Colin as he shuffled the pack of slipping black dominoes, 'what's tha' ganin' to do ti morn'?'

'Stay in bed!' interjected Fred with a laugh.

'No chance, Fred,' I replied. 'But I'm not sure, probably Cornelian or Castey.'

'Where t' 'ell is Cornelian?' asked Alan, picking up his six dominoes.

'Near Scarborough,' I replied. 'Come on Fred, it's your round.'

'Aye,' said Fred, 'tha' knows which'll fish best, don't tha'?' Putting four cream-topped amber pints on the table.

'Well …' I began to reply, but got no further.

'Blockhouse, from two hours afore to, well, two hours after high water.'

'Then move round towards Holbeck?' I asked.

'Aye, we could do, but unless this sea drops off a ton, ah don't reckon tha'll be able to fish Holbeck. No, we'll start at NALGO an' then go on ti blockhouse after,' he replied.

'Fred, you're on.'

So it was that the next day we arrived at the cinder track that leads to the car park above Cornelian, a little after noon on a bitter cold, grey day. It was cold. A raw cold that clung to you and made your limbs feel like sticks. The gale of the previous day had relented and given way to a fresh wind that hurried between the stark black trees that flanked the cliff top, curling back the withered yellow grass that grew there. Although it was early afternoon the premature grey of dusk was in the sky; to our left the lowering clouds and still restless sea fused in an obscure line that was ever shifting, as fine flurries of snow rose and spiralled from its surface, giving the whole scene a look of an arctic wilderness. As we walked, below us Cornelian Bay lay almost bare before the coming flood tide, its scars of rock black and pronounced against the grey of the sea.

Cornelian, as it is generally known, lies to the south of Scarborough: a small bay – a recess almost – within the line of sandstone cliffs that lie above and behind it. A narrow shelving beach separates the bottom of the cliff from an area of broken rocky scar. The scar itself is divided along its length by a deep gully that runs between the scars to join the sea at either end. The beach itself is almost in three parts: a large concrete blockhouse (a reminder of World War II) straddles the beach at its northern end, while to the south a slip of cliff had pushed a nab of rock and boulder clay out across the beach. It was our intention to fish from both the nab, and as the tide came onto high water, we would move to the blockhouse.

By the time we had reached the cliff bottom it was half tide, and a small surf was beginning to run on the beach, but there was still nowhere near enough depth of water inside of the scar to enable us to fish, so we leisurely began to get ourselves organised. It is to me always a reflective time, this time of preparation. It can be a very good moment inasmuch as all the major decisions relevant to the coming action have been taken, and as you pass line through rod rings you can look at the spot you have chosen and see if the signs are that it will keep its hoped-for promise.

As I stood there and looked at that heaving horizon, I had no doubts at all: every sign was good, from the grey overcast sky to the tumult of the sea, to the instinct born of the experience of time, that literally screamed at you that the Cod would be there, but in their time and not yours.

'By 'ell, Norman, I fancy this 'ole, an' yon blockhouse ternight,' said Fred as he proffered me one of his guaranteed-to-give-you-a-hole-in-your-lungs cigarettes.

'Yeah, it looks bloody marvellous, don't it, but I reckon we'll have to be canny as the sea gets over that scar cos there won't be any protection from the full force of that sea tonight.'

'Aye,' was his short reply.

Fred's cigarette lived up to its usual promise, and as I tried to get my breath back Fred decided to do his usual spot of 'scratting', that keen national pastime of looking along the high-water mark for that occasionally found valuable bit of flotsam.

I pressed on with my preparation, and when I had finished I sat down to watch and wait. We did not have to wait long, for the sea was still running high and it was as big a tide as the previous day. With each passing minute the depth of water at the bottom of the shelving beach rose visibly, and with the increase in depth the size of the running surf was growing in grandeur. The scar itself, 90 yards in front of us, was awash; the high curling rollers that had long assaulted it had triumphed, and now swept across the desolate scar unhindered. Now was the time to start, and as I began to bait up I saw that Fred, his search over, was hurriedly making his way back along the beach. Our bait, though two days old, was still in fine trim: big black lug that would stand the punch of the cast with little trouble, and stay firm on the hook.

I crossed the rapidly narrowing strip of sand, saw the spot where I wanted the bait to lie, and hit the ABU firmly. The lead swung away, high and straight, to land tight against the scar's edge, 90 yards to my left. I waded back to the dry beach, keeping the rod tip high and the line as tight as the wind that was straight off the sea would allow. I put the ABU multiplier into gear and stood the rod in its rest. I turned and saw that Fred too had now cast, but he had decided to put his bait more to our right where the scar swung seawards, and a good bit farther off than where mine lay.

A half hour went by, its passing only signified by our retreat before the ever-encroaching tide. The rod tips were unmoving, other than to the movement of the wind that grew colder as the light began to fade. Quick showers of snow and hail came upon us, hiding everything under their all-enveloping shroud of white. We reeled in the untouched baits and recast, each of us finding the spots we had had before, and continued to wait.

'It's still over early yet, Norman, not to worry,' said Fred, as he moved his gear up onto the nab that was going to be the first of our two platforms for the coming high water.

'Impatient, not worried,' I replied.

'Nay, surely not impatient,' said Fred, a harsh sarcasm etching his words. 'Why, we've only 'ad a forty-eight-hour wait, that's no reason ti' get impatient.' Then, as an afterthought, he looked at the growing tumult of water that now confronted us, and yelled out loud at the sea, 'C'mon! Where the 'ell are yer?'

Almost as the words were out of his mouth the line from my rod tip fell slack. I leapt across to the rod, dragging it from its rest, and began to walk backwards up the grass-topped nab. The line visibly tightened, and reeling hard, I swept the rod back. It came back in a long curve, stopping only as the hook hit something very solid out in the growing run of tide. After an initial dead stop, I began to get it moving towards me, but with each yard gained the fish was going farther away to my right so that I was fighting both the weight of fish and the full run of the tide upon it. Pumping the rod hard, and reeling when I could, I eventually got the fish to within 10 yards of the cliff bottom away to my right, and 12 feet below me. As a broken wave receded, we saw it: a Codling of 5 lb, its dorsal fins erect in the now shallowing water.

'I'll gerrit!' yelled Fred, running down the small narrow path that led from the nab where we stood, on to the beach below us.

'For pity's sake be careful!' I shouted at him and he raised his hand in acknowledgement of my cry.

Fred sprang from the path and sprinted across the ankle-deep sand; he reached the fish, bent down and pushed his fingers into its open gill case, lifted it and began to run back to the path. It was at this instant that I saw the wave coming. It rose high and curling, its grey-white tip arching high over Fred's head.

'Look out!' I screamed to him.

He did not look up but kept running, dragging the line from my rod behind him, the lead drawing a thin line of spray in the surface of the shallow water, shadowed by the now falling wave. He reached the bottom of the path and leapt for the safety of the small bank top. He could not do it: the wave fell with an almighty roar almost on top of him, the welter of spray and wave rose with alarming speed and Fred disappeared within it.

My heart stopped. I was numb with the horror of it. This could not be happening to us, it must be a mad dream from which I soon must surely wake. But I did not wake and I looked with stunned eyes as the sea climbed the short steep bank, carrying Fred within it. Then it fell back and Fred fell from the midst of the wave onto the streaming path. Even as I ran towards him I was too late, for yet another sea as big as the first crashed hard against the bank, rose with a roar like thunder and picked up the now-crouching Fred as though he were not there, and carried him high up the bank. Even as I looked, I saw Fred's right arm rise from the explosion of water that covered him, to grab at anything that was there. His fingers clawed the air, then caught around a small bunch of roots that projected from the bank from a long-dead tree that must have been buried in the nab below us. He held on; the water fell from him in a long angry fall of spray.

'My hand, Fred! Grab my bloody hand!' I reached out my hand to him and his fingers took mine. I heaved, and he came up onto the grass top.

'Bloody 'ellfire,' he croaked, his face running with water. 'Bloody 'ellfire, where the 'ell did that bugger come from?' He coughed long and hard, his whole body racked with the effort. 'Picked me up it did, just bloody well picked me up like I were just a bairn. Bloody 'ellfire.'

He straightened up, and from the depth of his arms he handed me the Codling.

'Next time thee can gan an' get thee own bloody fish.' He looked at me and smiled.

'You're lucky to be alive, Fred,' I answered, lighting up one of my own cigarettes and handing it to him.

'It'll take more'n a bloody bit o' sea to get me, mate. But that were over-close for comfort, too bloody close.'

We stood and looked at each other, laughing with relief.

'Well, after all mi efforts in't tha going to weigh it?'

I took out my scales and hung the fish from the brass hook.

'It weighs just over 5 lb, an' you got soaked for that. Weren't worth it.'

'Who got soaked?' asked Fred.

'Why you, of course,' I replied.

'Like 'ell I did. Just gotten a wet beard, that's all. Nowt else.'

'Ye gods, it's impossible not to have got soaked!'

'Aye, maybe, but I'll tell thee I'm dry.'

He was, too. Only his face and beard were wet, his oilskins and thigh-boots had served their purpose well.

'C'mon, then, ah reckon we'd better move on to blockhouse, ah don't fancy trying to land a big un 'ere now.'

So we moved. The trip to the blockhouse was not without its perils, with the sea now continually crashing up against the cliff bottom, but after Fred's escapade it was something of an anticlimax. From out of the dark ahead of us rose the blockhouse, the black finger of rock upon which it stood partially visible as the heaving surf fell back from its savage assault. We climbed the side of the cliff

179

that flanked its landward end, and walked out onto the pier-like top of the blockhouse. The top of the blockhouse was 12 feet above the sea and in many ways was a deal more dangerous than the place we had just left, but it had the security of concrete and steel, which in view of what had gone before was an improvement.

'We should be able to blast a good un off from 'ere,' I said.

'Aye. I fancy this spot Norman, I allus 'ave, for as long as ah can remember. There's been some good fish got and lost 'ere, an all; aye, real good uns.'

He put the Tilley lamp high on the cliff side that rose behind us, its bright yellow light spreading a comforting glow around us. He came back onto the top of the blockhouse, picked up his rod, and prepared to cast. I stood back and watched. For a man who had recently had a more than fortunate escape, Fred certainly did not show it. He leaned back, pushing his ABU rod away from himself, the lead swinging out towards the cliff, then stopping at the top of its arc, to curl back towards him. He dropped his wrists and the lead began to fall away again towards the cliff, but this time at speed. He turned his body, pulling the rod hard round, the compression now clearly showing, then the lead had gone, and the rod was pointing high into the darkness.

'Good un, that, a good un,' he said, moving across the concrete towards me.

I moved around the back of him and then I cast. It, too, was long, but as I took in the bow of slack line I found that I had pushed the lead over to the right. We stood side by side, our rods held upright against our bodies, fingers crooked around the line, not talking, aware of the sea, and its enfolding darkness. We must have stood like that for 20 minutes, the only sound that of the sea as it roared and pounded the concrete beneath us. Then Fred's rod was almost pulled from his arms, the tip was yanked down violently, the butt swinging upwards with near-equal force. Fred reacted quickly, dropping the rod tip, reaching at the same time for the large handle of the 9000. Reeling hard, Fred swept the rod back hard over his left shoulder, and gave a sudden exclamation of surprise.

'Yers, by 'ell a good fish.'

By the light of the yellow Tilley I could see that the rod was curved hard over, the tip dancing up and down as it followed the surge and rush of the hooked fish out there in that black night.

'He's comin'. Slow like, but comin'.'

'Big un?' I asked.

'Nay, but he'll do.'

I put down my rod, letting the tip project out over the edge of the blockhouse, put on my headlamp and made my way down onto the rocky scar that ran below.

'He's coming in now,' came a cry from above me.

I looked, and in the combined glow of both the Tilley and my headlamp I saw glinting line and below, in a foam-topped table of water, I saw the erect dorsal fins of a good fish. Fred swung his rod down towards me and I reached up and took the line into my left hand, trying to keep one eye on that fish that was beginning to go hard downtide.

'You got it, Norman?' yelled Fred.

'Not yet, give us a chance, damn it.'

Slowly, I began to get the fish coming towards me. It had almost reached the edge of the scar at my feet when a sea went by, taking the fish with it.

'Steady, Norman, steady,' came the voice above.

'I'll have 'im this time, no messing.'

I did, too. As the sea began its run back down the beach I again drew the line towards me, and this time it came easily, the Cod lying over on its side. I dropped down into the now quickly shallowing surf, put my hand under the gaping gill case, and lifted him out.

'Run, Norman, tha's another big un a'coming.'

I ran towards that scar like there was no tomorrow.

As I reached the blockhouse top Fred took the spragg from me, and weighed it. It went just over 7½ lb, a deep-flanked, grey-backed and white-bellied Cod that is typical of our winter fishing.

'I thought he'd go better than that; he looked nearer nine pound from up here,' said Fred wistfully.

'I remember reading somewhere that fish this size go better than twenty-pounders,' I said quietly.

'Aye, but then tha' doesn't want to believe all tha' reads. 'Ell, a chance ter get among such fish'd be a fine thing, imagine a twenty-pounder out there in that lot.'

The very idea was enough to make your blood run cold.

'Anyway Fred, c'mon, he's probably the first of many. Get yourself organised and get in again.'

He did, but we never had another touch. We fished for another two hours amid snow showers that were becoming more persistent, until we could stand the cold no longer.

'C'mon Fred, let me buy you a pint.'

'A game of dominoes an' all?'

'But of course.'

Binks and Castey

The summer of 1973 was memorable for a piece of fishing that in my experience was somewhat unique. On Saturday, 19th August 1973 I went Mackerelling on the Brigg, all to no avail. My wife's cousin, Howard, who was on the Brigg 'scrattin' for lost fishing tackle, had found two small soft green-backed shore crabs and offered them to me for immediate use.

I had always wanted to float fish a big softie crab down the bottom end of Binks, but for a number of reasons had never been able to do so. For one reason above all else: this particular spot is very popular for anglers ledgering, be it summer or winter. Not only that but in summertime there is another problem for anglers and that is the local and visiting sub aqua clubs who have a great interest in diving around the back of Filey Brigg. On this particular Saturday there was no one at all either fishing Binks or diving in or near it. It was a golden opportunity.

An hour before low water I set up my float tackle: my Spindrift rod, with a Mitchell 411 fixed spool reel laden with 8 lb breaking strain line, a long-bodied cork float set to slide and to fish 18 feet deep with two small soft crabs mounted on a size 5/0 Cannelle hook (not the ideal hook in these circumstances, but the only ones in my tackle box).

My first cast produced nothing at all, so the bait was restored to at least a presentable offering, and now at last I was able to get right down to the bottom of Binks. I cast as hard as I dare and put the bait 50 yards off the scar's edge. Within a few minutes it had drifted directly into the hole that is the main attraction for anglers on Binks.

My diary states:

After about ten minutes, down went the float. Truly, even
though I knew the idea would work, at the disappearance of
the float I just could not believe what was happening. This
pause in my response was invaluable as I was using soft crab
and you have to give the fish time to take the whole bait and
thus the hook into its mouth. I struck! The float came up, barely
visible; it was a good 50 yards away at the very least, then it
disappeared again. The rod keeled over and then began a five-
minute battle of which I can remember only momentary
snatches. Pumping, reeling, pumping again and again and slowly
recovering the 8 lb test line, I did not dare think about the line
especially here with its kelp patches, and razor-edged rock scars.
Then I got the fish directly under my feet. I saw it: a slight patch
of white and brown deep down in the green-blue water; up it
came slowly but surely until it wallowed in the slight lift of the
sea at the scar's edge. There was a difficult period whilst it was
gaffed by Howard who had been using his gaff as part of his
'scrattin' exercises, and we had it!

It weighed 8 lb 2 oz, taken on 8lb line at the bottom of Binks. It was
a minor triumph and I was, as I said at the time, 'well chuffed'!

The winter season of 1973/74 was again shared with Fred and
Noddy but like the curate's egg was only good in parts. The total
catch for the period 13th October 1973 to mid-April 1974 was
201 lb. Of this I took 123 lb, Fred 35 lb in only five trips, while
Noddy took 32 lb in eight trips. The fish of the winter was one of
mine taken at the north end of Castey Beach on a single salted
lugworm that went just over 12 lb. That was a memorable day for a
number of reasons.

Shortly after I had taken my fish I noticed that I had company.
Another angler was standing waiting for the tide to ebb to give access
onto the first 'runling' at the north end of Castey Beach. I knew him
by sight but could not recall his name; for the sake of what was to

follow I shall call him Don. Eventually the tide ebbed sufficiently so that we could continue fishing, but despite the amount of tidal water still covering the runlings the fishing was disappointing. We both fished between Green and Sunk Islands on the first of the larger runlings when Don had a good bite, struck, and landed a Cod of 13 lb 10 oz in absolutely mint condition. What I remember best of that moment was that Don reeled the fish in as if it were no more than a lump of weed, such was the strength of his tackle.

At exactly the same time that Don got into his fish, I too got into a 3½ lb Codling, that went well. I was still playing and battling with my more modest Codling as Don was landing his own fish; it was a good couple of minutes before I had landed mine. What made the moment memorable apart from the sight of seeing a double-figure Cod being caught and landed was that Don was using an 8-inch Scarborough reel with at least 50 lb b.s. monofilament line, a 13-foot long two-piece lancewood rod, a combination that would have landed a hundredweight bag of coal without incident.

Things quietened off immediately after that and, as these things happen, we got into conversation. I mentioned the fact that Castey was one amazing place, and dangerous despite its fascination. Don heard me out, and after a moment's pause told me a story that illustrated exactly the dangers of rock fishing, especially at night and, in the instance of his story, when it was foggy – and involved Castey.

But first I must try and describe Castey. Halfway between Scarborough and Filey is Cayton Bay. Although this is the east coast of Yorkshire, the coastline from Scarborough to Filey Brigg runs west to east, almost in a straight line. Cayton Bay lies on this line and the east headland of this small, open bay is called Yon's Nab. From Yon's Nab to the next inlet bay along the coast (called Chimney Hole) is an area of about 800 yards in length and some 200 yards in width when fully exposed at low water. This area of the Yorkshire coast is called Castey, and it offers just about everything anyone with an interest in nature, biology, birds, the sea or fishing would ever want to deal with in a lifetime. It is a fascinating place, of mixed ground, with a sandy beach flanking deep gullies of rock scars and boulders that run east to west in parallel lines to the beach, locally called 'Runlings'. There is the wreckage of lost trawlers, ship's boilers, deep and wide holes and gullies that are full of water even at low tide. This is a very dangerous place, where it is so easy to be cut off on some outlying scar with difficult if not impossible means of escape, especially after dark. No one unaware of Castey's perils should ever go there unaccompanied or children unsupervised – to do so is only asking for trouble with a capital T. Most of Castey has local names: Green Island, Sunk Island, Dyke, Tins, Wrasse Hole and Pudding Hole, to name but a few. As you would expect, a number of ships have been lost to this hazardous coastline over the last four hundred years and their remains are still evident. Overlooking this mystery of sea, sand, rock and deep holes are majestic cliffs that add an aura to it all. Be in no doubt, to get to know Castey is a lifetime's work, particularly how the tides work on the flood and ebb, and even today there are a few locals who work this area with single pots for crabs and lobsters who would be the first to admit that despite many years of effort, they are still learning the foibles of this place every time they go there. Anyway, that is Castey, and so we have Don and his story.

Don decided that the big tides of one particular autumn were worth a trip to fish Castey, particularly to fish Outscar, that line of rock edge that separates Castey from the deep sea beyond. He would not go alone but with his brother-in-law, and they would fish it overnight. On the night it was thick fog, frosty-cold and windless, but they found their way to Outscar and the place they had fished from once before: they were full of optimism for their prospects.

This particular spot has a 'warning rock': when the tide is in flood the sea so laps the underside of the rock that the noise is unmistakable, and you get out of there as soon as possible. This fact they knew, and so they set about their task. They had had some good fish and were a bit tired when the rock began its warning lap, and so they packed up their gear and set off for the beach, the car and home. By now it was very cold, and if anything the fog was worse than before they had arrived.

They had been walking for 15 minutes or so and had begun to

wonder when the familiar rocky marks would start to appear, thus giving them a guide as to how far they had come, but they had seen nothing familiar at all. Then, suddenly, they were all but knee-deep in water and before them in the light of their head lamps were all the signs of their earlier occupation of the place they had fished and just left minutes before. Floating newspapers that had held their bait, the debris of the gutted fish, but more concerning was the sight of the lapping rock. It was now under water! They had walked around in a circle, had missed all the points of navigation, and were in immediate danger of being cut off from their means of escape, and in danger of their lives.

The conversation between Don and his brother-in-law can only be imagined: expressions of disbelief and probably no little censure of Don for his failure to get them off the scar safely. Don went on to tell me that he decided there and then that they had only one means of escape, and that was to turn their backs directly to the open sea and walk in as near as possible a straight line to the shore 200 yards away, regardless of what they came across on the way; if they had to swim, then they had to swim. This was met with silence and then agreement. So, that is what they did.

Whereas the rocky scars that make up the runlings are for the most part exposed at low tide, the areas between the scars for the most part remain filled with water. The further from the shore the runling, the deeper the water that flanks it and it is wider than those runlings closer to the beach. They walked for a few yards and then met their first runnling; the prospect of what this must have meant to both of them can only be imagined. Did they jump in or climb down into the water? What about the rods? The tackle bags? The caught fish? And all the time the sound of the incoming tide would have been assaulting their ears, reminding them of the ever-increasing risk to their lives.

Don said that neither he nor his brother-in-law were good swimmers; in fact Don did not know just what he was going to do. Once in the first runling their decision as to what to do was made for them: swim! It was deep and very cold. They doggy-paddled their way across, relinquishing their baggage as they crossed to the other side where they found the rocky scar now awash. They stumbled across the rock scar, trying desparately not to slip or fall over, somehow keeping going despite being soaked and getting ever colder despite their efforts.

Then they came on the next runling and it was back into the water again; this was as deep as the first and even wider, but they got across and were now aware that they were becoming physically tired. After all they were no longer young men, both of them had done a day's work prior to going fishing, and it could hardly have surprised either of them that their energy was all but gone. The fog was as thick as before, so they had no idea how far they had come, nor any idea how far they had to go, and the dread of a very wide and deep runling was looming ever larger in their thoughts.

And so they went on. Don could not remember how many runlings they had had to swim across, but eventually they had only to wade, and then finally paddle, and then they were on the beach. They had no idea where they were on the beach, a beach that has only two cliff pathways in all of Castey's length that give access, which they had to find to get up the cliffs and to their car.

Nor did Don remember just how long they sat on the beach getting themselves back together sufficiently to find the path and then climb the cliffs. Eventually they set off, aware that if they continued to stay where they were they'd probably be done for either by hypothermia or the fast-rising tide. They had the presence of mind to conclude that they had to go to their right, northwards, since the cliffs at the Redcliff end of the beach were somewhat easier to climb than at the south end, at Chimney Hole. After a difficult, stumbling walk along a debris-strewn beach they found the bit of cliff that gave access to the path. Fearing that if they stopped for breath now they'd never climb the pathway, they pressed on. By the time they got to their car they were no longer frozen, but utterly, completely exhausted.

They drove home in silence. Don dropped his brother-in-law off first and then drove the few further miles home. He spent the next two hours in a bath, just getting warm. And no doubt giving thanks for their amazing escape. A dire warning to us all.

Don and I fished on as the runling before us continued to empty, until I called it a day and went home, still pondering on Don's amazing escape and whether I would have had such courage to have done what he and his companion did that foggy, frost-bound morning. I hope I never have to find out.

Escapes like that are rare, but do happen. In my own lifetime I have had one or two hairy moments, but nothing like what happened to Don and his companion. Once I got onto the back of the Brigg on a fine evening, but within an hour it had begun to rain, and rain heavily. It had been a humid day anyway but with the rain it was now very humid. I had gone to spin for Mackerel and was fishing from Ling Rock. On what must have been my fifth or sixth cast of the night I had an electric shock that felt like somebody had hit my right arm with a club, and I tingled everywhere. I just could not believe what had happened to me. Why, when it was obvious to an idiot what had happened, I cast again … This time it was even worse and I dropped the rod, so painful was the shock. Some anglers fishing nearby who were watching me said that I had glowed a soft lime green, and the second time it was even brighter, and for a moment they thought I'd bought it!

Then there are the unexpected waves …

Freak Waves

In September 1995, RMS *Queen Elizabeth II*, whilst crossing the North Atlantic, encountered what is usually called a freak wave, 95 feet high, a product it was believed at the time of Hurricane Luis. The Master said, 'it came out of the darkness ... looked like the White Cliffs of Dover', and resultant newspaper reports described the cruise liner as attempting to 'surf' the near-vertical wave in an attempt not to be sunk! There are many other such reports going back to the nineteenth century and I have no doubts that such waves have been occurring since time immemorial. Obviously, my experience of freak waves comes nowhere near such a wave as hit the QE2, but they were nonetheless big enough to scare me.

Many anglers can go through their sea fishing career and never either see such a wave or (Heaven forbid!) actually experience one. It is very probable that those who have experienced such a freak wave, or a lesser-sized but still huge and dangerous wave, did not survive the experience. In my fishing lifetime I experienced three large waves, and although all three did vary in size they were nonetheless terrifying moments, never forgotten.

The first time was at a place called Iron Scar, a fishing spot located about halfway between Cloughton and Hayburn Wyke, 10 miles north of Scarborough. Iron Scar, despite the long and difficult walk from Cloughton Wyke, was once a popular spot for anglers. A large, flat slab of pitted and holed sandstone rock, flanked on either side by large sandstone boulders, typical of much of the coastline between Filey Brigg and Saltburn-by-the-Sea, in Cleveland, Iron Scar is about 10 feet above sea level. It slopes towards the sea from the cliff foot and is canted so that the south side of the slab is a little lower than its northern edge. Its flatness provides part of the attraction in that the flatness of the scar provides a much better casting platform than the boulder-strewn cliff foot. Its other attraction is that it is a difficult place to get to, so that relatively fewer anglers visit compared to other places locally, and it follows that it may hold a head of fish unused to baits and the like. That is the argument, anyway, and was one of the reasons that six of us made the long and arduous walk to fish Iron Scar on the last day of the FBAS Festival, the North of England Codling Championship.

It was a fine and sunny day, cloudless and warm, the sea slight, more a day for enjoying the garden or the beach with family and friends than going 'Cod bashing'. Three hours after casting our baits only one fish had been caught, a rich red-flanked 4 lb in weight 'native' Codling, so called locally because the fish had spent some time living and feeding in the kelp (known locally as 'tangles') that pervade this coastline, and in doing so had adopted the colour of the weedy environment that sustained it.

I saw it first. A long, darkish line on the surface of the sea, a shadow, like a line of smoke that was coming towards the shoreline from a what seemed to be a long way off. I kept watching it, a bit bemused, for I had never seen anything like this before in my life and to be honest was a little reluctant to say anything. But as I watched it became obvious that it was not smoke, but a wave, and coming very quickly towards us. It was lifting as it did so, underlining that it was a wave. I yelled, and very quickly six rods were being lifted and line let out and then all six of us were running as fast as our rods would allow us, back up the scar towards where our gear, bags and rucksacks were laid on the highest point of the scar.

I had that very morning bought a new oilskin and a strawbag to hold it, and my other bag contained my precious camera as well as my tackle boxes, lunch box and so on. The wave hit and came up that scar waist-deep and travelling like an express train. It went through me and picked up both of my bags as it continued its journey to the cliff foot.

I grabbed at one of my two strawbags; the other was gone in an instant. I had no time to look to my friends for help for they were as involved in survival as I was, and that strawbag was lost for sure. Using the butt of my rod as a support I pushed it down as hard as I could onto the slab beneath me, and the rod held. I was at least safe. I now saw that what was left of the wave was going back down the scar to the sea that had given it birth. In the midst of that maelstrom was one of my strawbags. I could do nothing whatsoever except to hold on until all the water had gone. I had picked up the strawbag with my camera and the rest of my gear so I was pretty much relieved, but sore at the loss of the coat, which had been expensive, especially for someone on my salary scale.

We all survived, but we were well and truly shaken up by what had happened. And soaked from the waist down, despite all of us wearing waders. The walk back to our cars was made in silence. It was only afterwards when talking about it at our local pub that we realised: if that wave had washed over any one of us and then taken him back out to sea with its backwash, just how could we have got help of any kind, bearing in mind just how isolated a place Iron Scar was? No mobile phones in those days! Despite John's fish winning a prize, the wave had more than coloured our day and etched itself in memory.

The second big wave in my life was while fishing the Boxing Day Match, one of FBAS's Christmas events to keep members busy over the festive season. It was very much the same group who had fished at Iron Scar that September day, plus a couple of others, and we were fishing Green Rock, a popular spot both winter and summer on the back of Filey Brigg close by the safety ladder. The back of the Brigg is a series of steps that begin at the cliff foot, beginning with an access pathway 8 feet wide, then two steps down over about 6 feet onto a sloping flat scar 5 yards wide. This flat scar slopes upwards towards the sea's edge, which at low water is about 10 feet above the sea. Its openness makes it popular with everyone, providing space for casting and for a number of rods to stand side by side.

It was a grey day, fully overcast, and it was cold enough to hold the threat of snow at any time. The tide was making and the sea state was what locals call 'jowly', a moderate swell, enough to keep you on your toes to run whenever a wave appeared that threatened to crash across the flat scar we were fishing from. There was just enough sea on as to make it questionable as to whether we should be fishing there at all, but being young and daft enough not even to consider such a sensible question, the question was never raised. We were all fishless; there had not even been a bite, and our enthusiasm for the match and the day was fast disappearing. I had just reeled my gear in, and was standing at the bottom of the two 'steps' with my back to the sea looking at my bait, a black lugworm in much the same state as it had been when I had cast it out 20 minutes before. I stood there trying to make up my mind whether to pack up and go home or have one more cast.

Suddenly there was a loud shout from above me.

'Look out! There's a wave, a big un! Look out, Fred!'

I turned to look towards the scar's edge where half a dozen rods were all standing, their butts pushed into holes cut and chiselled out of the rock edge to form rod holes. Fred was already running towards the rods, but beyond him, 30 yards seaward of Green Rock, was a wall of water, grey-black, foam-flecked and the peak of it curling over as it began its fall onto the scar's edge.

Fred grabbed as many of the rods as his reach allowed, and hunching over turned his back to the sea and awaited the deluge. At that very moment Ian Parrish set off from where he had been standing in the middle of the scar, towards the remaining upright rods.

'Ahm coming, Fred!' he yelled at the top of his voice.

'Ian, get the hell out of there!' chorused the rest of us, to no avail.

All the while the wall of water had continued its journey and now crashed into the vertical face of the scar that was Green Rock, and went up and over Fred who disappeared in the welter of foam and water. Ian, meanwhile, had moved barely at all; it seemed as if the shouts of warning had had an effect for he suddenly stopped in his run, becoming very much aware of what was happening and what was about to happen to him. The wave hit Ian full on, and like a well-hit skittle all 6 feet of him was bowled over. Before we had time to even blink he was being carried away from us as the wave then hit the foot of the stepped rockway and turned back on itself to travel at speed past me, head-high, as it swept down the full length of the scar towards the end of the Brigg, well away to our right. We all just stopped and stared.

Ian, flat on his back, was carried like a piece of flotsam in a mill race. His arms waved, but there was nothing whatever he could do, lying as he was on about 3 feet of fast-moving seawater.

Finally, the water at our feet abated. Fred staggered down towards us, dripping wet but with no other problems, and more or less as one we all set off along the scar towards Ling Rock. Then suddenly the water supporting Ian just vanished and Ian was dumped, bodily and heavily, onto the flat scar 80 metres from where he had been picked up by the wave. As we ran towards him, Ian stood up and it seemed as if half of the North Sea poured from out of his waterproof clothing.

'You alright?'

'Think so,' said Ian and began coughing. 'Yeah, I'm alright.'

'You lucky bastard, Ian! Have you any idea …? Your head missed the scar edges and sides of t' Brigg as if by magic. Amazin'. Bloody amazin'!'

'You've been dead lucky, Ian, you've no idea …'

'Hell's teeth, I'm bloody frozen!' replied Ian. 'How am I going to get home like this?'

No one spoke. Then from the top of the safety ladder came a lone voice, but loud enough not to be missed.

'Parrish! Get yer gear together and get yer sen up here. Ah've got me bike at top of cliff and ah'll give thee a lift 'ome!' It was George Burton, a local character of renown who had come onto the Brigg for an afternoon walk.

Ian, as best he could with help from all of us, got himself together and set off to the safety ladder and George's lift home. As he left I looked about me; everything was just as it had been only a few minutes ago. Fred was wet and Ian had escaped a dreadful fate, but to look about us it was if nothing whatsoever had happened at all. A wave? What wave?

Writing about this almost 50 years after it happened, I can still see that wave in my mind's eye, still feel that sense of fear as I saw the wave coming and the disbelief and huge relief of Ian's escape.

The third experience of a huge wave was some time later, and compared to the other two was a deal more scary. This time I was not fishing, but walking our two dogs on Filey beach, a lonely place in the dark of winter. We had two dogs in our household in those days, an Afghan Hound we had christened Plod as a result of certain events that had happened in our courting days, and a Bearded Collie called Ross after a Cornish novel and its hero. (That we had a cat as well who was the absolute ruler of the house may well be true but it has nothing to do with this story, except to say that she made our home an interesting place to live.)

For most of the year the dogs were walked by my wife, excepting for those months that were particularly snowy, gale-torn or ravished by heavy rain, especially in darkness. Julie managed well in the daylight but when the weather really did break she preferred that I took them when the bad weather coincided with darkness.

This arrangement worked well, for I loved such hard weather and over the years I had put together a routine of walks so that once we set out, the dogs knew exactly where we would be going. In all these walks the Affie would disappear into the night only to be seen as a shadow darker than the background as he worked his way along our route, always looking for a smell sweeter than the rest. At times Plod could be 300 or even 400 yards from where I was, running along the cliff foot, or making his way up the cliffs, or running like the wind from one fairway to another on the local golf course in pursuit of the last vestiges of the scent of the local fox. Always, if you looked closely, you could see him; it was just a question of a tuned eye born out of many years of walking him in darkness. As for Ross, all he wanted was a stick as big as he was, that he could carry for the full length of the walk with all the resulting incidents that a mobile tree trunk usually produced.

This particular evening was at the beginning of a week of big tides, a week that had also seen the first real edges of winter. A fresh northerly wind had produced a big sea as well as squalls of hail, sleet and snow. High tide that afternoon had been gone for a good three hours by the time the three of us reached the beach. No sooner had Plod been released from his lead than he was off into the dark, running along the high-tide mark of the cliff foot 100 yards or more to my right. Ross as usual had brought his tree trunk with him and once free of his lead set about rounding me up with typical collie zeal.

I made my way south along the beach, away from the yellow glimmer of the sea wall lights, into the darkness of the sea and cliffs. It was particularly dark that evening, as it always is immediately before the moon is set to rise, a darkness that seemed all the more enveloping with the flurries of rain and sleet obscuring even the distant coastal lights. I looked to my left at the sea, the white curl of the falling breakers stark against the even darker mantle of the sea itself, with no line between the sea's distant edge and the heavy, brooding sky, I remember thinking that I was glad that the ebb was set full now, as it would have been difficult to judge its speed of flow across the beach had the tide been flooding.

We had walked for about five minutes, with Ross continually at my feet defying me to try and grab his stick, when from out of the dark of the cliff to my right came Plod, running as if the Devil himself was after him. So quickly did he appear that Ross forsook his stick to respond to this arrival, barking with even more enthusiasm than was his wont. Plod ran around us, barking as he did so, and for a moment I thought he must be jealous of Ross and his continual involvement with me, to the extent that I often had little time for the Afghan. I yelled at him to stop and even tried to grab him as he sped past me and this combined with the frantic attempts for Ross to get in on the act made the whole scene a whirligig of noise and running dogs.

By now I was utterly bemused and had no idea what Plod was getting so excited about. I realised too that if it had been an act of jealousy then Plod would surely have driven Ross off, but he made no such attempt. Plod suddenly stopped his crazy circling run, skidding to a halt between me and the sea. There, with his front legs stretched out before him, his backside high in the air, he barked that bark that he only ever made when there was danger, or someone or another dog that he especially disliked.

Still not comprehending just what he was about, I looked up for a moment beyond the dog – and saw the wave. For a moment I just froze. I just could neither grasp nor believe what my eyes were telling me. A hundred yards away, and coming up that beach like an express train, was a huge wall of water, a wave of such huge proportions that it was continuing to lift and curl over even as I watched. Plod leapt past me and I turned to follow as fast as I could. I have never run so fast before or since, and I doubt that even as a fit young man I could have run any faster than I did up that beach. I did not dare to look back, but just kept my eyes on the dark cliff ahead of me and hoped that when I got there I could readily climb up.

Ross, thinking this a grand game, tried to run about my feet, and my breathless response was in language that he could rarely have heard. By now the cliff was coming fast upon us and instinctively I followed the dark running form of the Afghan, now veering away to my right. I looked and saw that where he was heading for was a pathway up the cliff, a way I had forgotten about, so rarely had I used it. The noise from behind me now was that of running, breaking water, and I leapt for the cliff where the Afghan had run only moments before. I had not got more than 2 yards up that path, with Ross feverishly scratching at the path for a grip, when the sea hit the cliff foot with an almighty crash. The broken wave climbed the cliff face and snatched at my legs, soaking me almost to my waist.

The ice cold of the soaking stopped me dead in my tracks. At that moment the moon broke from behind its curtain of cloud to illuminate a quite awesome scene. From almost the end of the seawall 300 yards to my left, and as far as I could see to my right, the once bare beach was now covered by the sea, a heaving carpet of silver, black and grey shadows that for just a moment seemed fixed to the beach by an enormous pin, so little did it seem to move. Then with a uniformity of movement that filled me with no little fear it began to retreat back down the beach from whence it came. So fast was its retreat that waves were formed by its backwash and the chatter of shingle and rocks made an eerie cacophony of sound, like someone sucking the very dregs of life from a reluctant victim.

I stood there for some time until at last the sea's edge was maintained along the line of tide that it had reached before that rogue wave made its appearance. I had heard of rogue waves and recalled the one that swept Iron Scar clean of everything upon it, a scar 10 feet above the sea on a day as calm and as flat as an ironing board. Like that, this wave had come from nowhere, but whereas that wave of old had risen a mere 10 feet from a flat calm sea, this one must have been 15 feet high and had run at least 150 yards beyond the boundary of that ebbing tide to crash against the cliff foot with a violence and malevolence that took my breath away.

'Plod!' I called out to the Afghan. 'C'mon to me, there's a good dog. How did you know? Plod, just how did you know?'

He came back down the cliff towards me and I, gently patting the nape of his neck, was completely disbelieving of what he had done, and how he had done it. I climbed back down onto the beach and in total silence continued my walk. Soon I came the point where I would leave the beach and climb up to the cliff top and the path for home. I was still numb, not believing what I had seen or heard, all of it. I reached the cliff top path and there sat upon the bench seat provided for visitors to enjoy the view. As I looked out across the bay the tide line had slipped even further down the beach and there was no sign whatever of the wave and its effects. It was as though it had never happened, a figment of my imagination, and for some time I did indeed doubt that it had happened. I stood and began to make my way back along the cliff path and towards home and beauty. All the usual routine parts of the walk continued to materialise, Ross finding another stick, Plod coming out of the black of the hills to be put upon his lead, and then at last the lights of the town and home was reached.

I tried very hard to tell Julie what had happened, and Plod's part in it, and she listened attentively. But to this day I do not know if she really believes me.

'Just how did he know, Julie?' I asked, as I was to ask many times hereafter.

'I don't really know, Nav. Not really, not if I'm honest.'

There is a footnote to this extraordinary story. Fifteen years later I was fishing on the back of Filey Brigg on a cold, grey November morning when I was joined on the flat scar of Green Rock by a group of anglers, very much visitors and all in their teens. After a very brief look around they set off to a new position to my left, making their way carefully down onto a flat scar that had now been exposed by the ebbing tide. It was obvious that these lads were full of youthful bravado and very much unaware of the dangers that the this exposed scar was subject to, for there was a good deal of lift from what locals would call a 'jowly' sea.

'Hey!' I shouted. 'Take care on that scar, there's a lot of lift!'

They looked up at me with no little suspicion, but stopped and looked at the sea and the scar and one of them shouted an acknowledgement of sorts that I barely heard. Then I was touched upon my arm, and turning around found that I had been joined by yet another angler but this one was much older than the others.

'Oh, hello,' I said. 'Are that lot with you, then?'

'No, not at all, don't know 'em. But I heard you warn 'em about the lift.'

'Aye,' I replied, 'there's a bit. It's falling off now as it's almost low water, but it can still be a bit hairy, you must always take care on here.'

He looked at me for a moment and shook his head. 'You don't have to tell me that!' he said. 'I almost lost my life on there.' He pointed towards High Nab, a headland of cliff with flat rock scars at its foot 100 yards away.

'I were fishing there all afternoon with ne'r a bite and decided that I'd give it a go after dark and fish the tide down, then I'd set off home about 8 o'clock regardless. Well, unknown to me some anglers began to fish from the cliff top directly above my head, bloody stupid of 'em, they must have seen my light below 'em, so I decided to pack up straight away … it just weren't safe there any more. And then suddenly I heard shouts and a flashing of lights all about me. I looked up and heard quite distinctly, 'Look out! There's a big wave!' He stopped talking and looked past me towards High Nab. A look passed across his face that it was not difficult to see was one of fear, even in remembrance.

'What happened?' I asked.

'I just had time to turn and look, my headlight picked out what could only be a wave. I saw the safety chain at the back of the scar tight against the cliff foot, and dived for it. I had no sooner got my hands on it than the wave hit the cliff, and me! I was flung to my left, I gripped that bit of chain with all my strength as the sea fell onto me and rushed off the scar back into the sea. It seemed to last for ever. But soon enough it had gone, leaving me soaked to the quick and all my tackle gone with the sea!'

He stopped talking and suddenly grabbed my arm and squeezed it hard.

'OK,' I said, 'no problem.' I could see that he was upset. 'Now tell me, when did this happen, what time of the year?'

He then told me that it was in late October or early November, 15 years ago, and as best he could remember at about seven in the evening. He went on to say that he'd got off High Nab and climbed the cliff back to his car in a state of shock, which in the circumstances was hardly surprising.

'You know,' I said, 'I had much the same kind of adventure on the beach …'

Winter Fishing, 1974/75

The winter fishing of 1974/75 was a watershed in a number of ways. My work was very much all-consuming. I had been working from home for almost ten years and as a result the extent of my work stretched far and wide across the north of England, including the occasional venture in London. This left me with less time than ever to pursue my fishing and since most of my fishing friends had all had life changes of one kind or another there was no one available to act as a spur for me to make that extra effort to go fishing. The next problem was the increase in the cost of petrol (65p per gallon; that it is ten times that today says much) which made a round trip to Hilston (about 116 miles all told and 2½ gallons of fuel) expensive. Fred Hall had got involved in a commercial shoot and so his weekends were now already decided. But there was one thing that materialised for me this winter, and that was that the level of my ignorance when it came to rock fishing.

So much time and effort had been expended in learning how to fish the beaches of Holderness that next to no thought at all had been made to learn, and more importantly understand, the intricacies of rock angling. If there was one question that we consistently failed to answer correctly, it was where do we go when the sea is rough and the beaches are unfishable? The choice of rock fishing venues was extensive, but to select the right spot was beyond us and we invariably went to the wrong place, albeit at the right time.

So: it is too rough to fish Holderness, so where do we go? To know that Castey would fish well may well be correct, but where to fish at Castey? That was the key to success, and that level of knowing was something that we just did not possess.

But I did go sea fishing, and between the beginning of October 1974 and the middle of March 1975 I caught 107½ lb of fish, including my very best fish from the shore taken at NALGO, a beach between the west side of Osgodby Nab, Cayton and Cornelian Bay, several hundred yards east of Scarborough's famous Spa complex. There were some amazing catches made over this winter with one Filey angler, Bob Brannan, taking 28½ lb in two fish from Cornelian Bay in late November (one fish was 18¼ lb), and then the catch of a lifetime for any angler anywhere. He took 12 Codling at Captain Flinton's Harbour (the north end of Cayton Bay beach) fished during the low-water period at night, a total weight of 63 lb, which is a Filey Brigg Angling Society competition record. The effort he made to get that weight of fish plus his tackle from the beach and up to the car on the cliff top road must have been back-breaking. If you think about it, it was a three-hour match; that means he took a fish every 15 minutes, and since the average weight of each fish was over 5 lb, the water flanking the scar Bob fished from must have been alive with fish!

Over the Christmas period and on the same day a Cod of 16¼ lb was taken at Cornelian Bay, and a fish of 20¾ lb was caught at Jackson's Bay, north of Scarborough. Meanwhile, Syd Gibson, fishing Redcliff Hole in Cayton Bay, took 43 lb of fish in four hours: he had three fish of 6 lb, one of 13 lb and one of 14 lb.

I must say something about my own 'best fish'. It was not without its lessons; maybe 'price' is a better word than 'lessons'. That is to say, it was not just a simple case of going, catching and coming home; the best fishing rarely is.

I had to get my bait at Fraisthorpe, some 18 miles south of Filey, on an ice-bound morning, with road surfaces all the way there and back that were dangerous with black ice. I was on that beach for 75 minutes and in that time found, but more importantly dug, three lugworm. Well, two lugworm (gullies) and one good blastie. Just three baits; that should have told me something was up, but it did not. To go fishing, Noddy was providing the transport, inevitably we were late in arriving on NALGO beach and decided to fish what we had called the Point. This is literally a nab of cliff, rising about 20 feet above the beach, about 130 yards from Osgodby Nab, fronted with a beach of sand that slopes quite steeply down to a rocky and small boulder-strewn gully that lies tight against a rock scar. This scar stretches most of the way from Osgodby Nab to Cornelian Bay. This rock scar is about 90 yards from the top of the nab, the scar itself being slightly raised above the gulley of small stones and rocks. It is a good cast with bait.

Noddy was sure I was wrong in my choice of spot but reluctantly agreed, and so we got ourselves organised. I had very little bait and so the timing of my fishing had to be very carefully considered, since on arrival it was three hours to high water. Nonetheless, the sea was already breaking across the highest point of the scars of rock to our left (locally called Clarke's Island) and the rocks in front of us were completely hidden with a moderate surf running. I cadged some of Noddy's salted lug but this time I had not a bite on what had often proved to be a good standby bait.

About an hour before high water I put on my best lugworm, and casting just to the right of the nab, I tried my best to try and reach the back of the gulley at its widest point. It was a good cast, dare I say so myself, and more importantly the bait held where it had dropped, so I had to be tight against the small scar edge.

The bite when it came was almost a non-starter. The rod tip dipped slightly, then again. On picking up the rod it felt as though the lead was being moved. 'Dropped' is a better way of describing it. Then the line slackened; I took in the slight amount of slack line. The lead knocked again. Then the rod tip dipped, oh ever so slightly, and I hit it hard. The rod came back fast and stopped almost dead in its arc, only to curve over steeply, and it dipped down hard.

My diary records what happened next: 'There was a moment's resistance, a somewhat heavy resistance and it came, if heavily.'

'Yes, I'm in, Noddy!'

But Noddy had gone, grabbing the gaff in his flight to the beach.

205

The sea had by now covered Clarke's Island and the wave runs had reached the cliff foot, though as yet there was little water there.

I pulled it 50 yards and it had come quite easily, and I felt that though it was a good fish it would go no more than 8 lb. I had no sooner thought this than the rod was almost pulled out of my hands, so vicious was the surge of the fish. It began to go hard uptide to my left, taking line against an almost full set drag, and I quickly jabbed my fingers onto the star drag to ease it off. It must have taken 10 to 15 yards of line before I got its head round.

Then 50 yards from the shoreline I saw the water boil, just for a moment, yet the image it formed was so clear that that 'boil' of water is etched on my memory still. I swore loudly. It was more a scream than an oath, but Noddy heard it, and for me it let off a lot of steam.

It went again and I got some of the line I had lost and some more again back on the reel. It was by now 10 yards from the back of the heavily breaking surf and now the fish went mad. Again it surged away but this time straight out, taking with it a good many yards of line and not easing the deep curve of my rod at all, but increasing it. My breath was laboured, my heart going incessantly, so loud it seemed I could almost hear its beat above the roar of the booming surf. I screamed at Noddy, now directly below me and a little to my right, to take great care with such a heavy surf now running at the cliff foot.

At that very moment the high arched back of the Cod broke water, the high dorsal fin cleaving the dark, tea-brown surface of the sea as the fish turned up and over the line, trying to break both line and trace. But I had the line taught; it broached again, giving rise to enormous screams from both Noddy and me.

'Its bloody ginormous!' I yelled.

Then the fish was in the tumbling, broken surges of the falling surf, the tension on the rod and line easing as the running surf carried the big fish well up the beach. Noddy, his momentary judgement clouded by the size of the fish and the excitement of the moment, began to wade towards the still very active big fish that was wallowing in the deep, long, table of surf.

'Wait!' I screamed at him.

It was a good job that I did, for the fish, sensing the nearness of the beach, took advantage of the run back of the wave and began to go out again towards the breaking surf and the deeper water. The next wave rose high above the fish, curled over and fell onto the fish with a great roar, the spume climbing quickly skyward and hiding all from view. As the wave lifted from its broken force it began its shoreward rush and again I got the fish coming in.

It was tired now and in the lull of the flow of the wave I saw it roll over, exposing an enormous white flank and a great tail.

'Its the biggest I've ever seen!' yelled Noddy, almost calmly, to which I screamed back a long-forgotten oath to get the hell out of my line of vision. Another wave ran in and I heaved hard and long and the fish turned and came, slowly at first then quicker.

'Now! Noddy, now!' I yelled as loud as my breathless body would allow.

He ran hard through the foam-flecked surface of the surf, swung the gaff and had the fish through the gills. Noddy gasped so loudly I could hear it from where I was. Another great wave had by now broken and begun its charge to the beach, and I yelled at Noddy to get the hell out of it, he was risking his life where he was. In his anxious scramble to drag the fish and himself from the surf he backed straight into a large boulder that stood like a sentinel at the cliff foot. He went flying, his boots coming clean out of the water, the gaff flying out of his hand in a great arcing sweep.

'Get the bloody gaff!' I shouted in disbelief.

He did, pulling himself upright at the same time, and then he ran, slipped and splashed through the dying surf, dragging the enormous fish behind him.

He scrambled up the path towards the top of the nab and handed me the gaff, his face wreathed in a great smile. I heaved up the fish onto the cliff top and could hardly believe my eyes. A deep-bodied Cod, with heavy sagging belly, bronze-flanked and golden-spotted with a stark white underside. It was the biggest Cod I had ever caught in my life; it had gone like the clappers, fought hard, disproving the old myth that Cod do not fight. This fish had fought hard for its life fom the moment it was hooked until it was lifted from the surf, and in that fight had made the catch memorable for life.

We fished on and with my last gullie I took another Codling, this time of just under 5 lb. It had been quite a day, and for me unforgettable. We went into Scarborough and had the fish officially weighed, at Pritchards Tackle Shop (the ever-patient Mr Edwin Peart). Five hours after being caught it went 18 lb 15 oz 14 drams. The story of its capture did not end there; after being photographed at home, during the process of developing the black and white film there was a total failure of the developer (I know not how … probably too old) which resulted in not one image being produced. The failure was such that I have no photos of the fish, save an image that is hardly worth the paper it was not printed on, and this despite pounds spent on gear!

I must say something about Noddy. Despite his fall, he had done a good job in gaffing my big fish; it is more than doubtful that had I been on my own with that sea running I would have been successful in landing it.

During the summer of 1975, Noddy, fishing a whole 6 inches across soft edible crab (and without a lead, the weight of the crab being enough, thought Noddy, to get the bait out far enough), fishing from the big flat scar that fronts Cock 'n' Hen Hole on the backside of Filey Brigg, after a long wait for the bait to be taken, he took and landed on his own a Cod of 14 lb 13½ oz. It was 33 inches long and in prime condition.

The following December, 1976, he went to NALGO and fished the self-same nab I had taken my big fish from, but this time Noddy was on his own. Again on his best cast of the day, he hooked and fought a good Cod that was just as spirited as mine had been earlier in the year. It was even more of a feat than was obvious, for as he dragged the fish up the beach as it lay on a run of a wave, the hook trace broke! Before the fish realised its good fortune, Noddy fell upon the fish, clutching both rod and fish to his chest, and this despite the fact that it was almost high water, with the sea a deal rougher than it had been when I had taken my big fish. The fish that weighed 14 lb 8 oz, his best winter fish for some time.

Both these fish and the manner of their capture say a great deal about Noddy's skill and wherewithal, because neither capture, especially the one at NALGO, was particularly easy, and both demanded no little courage in the sea conditions that prevailed.

A Disappointing End

The winter fishing of 1975/76 and 1976/77 were the most disappointing for me of any fishing period ever. It is enough to say that my work was more onerous than ever and now being a married man of some years had its own demands and responsibilities. I did go fishing, but things had changed in other ways too.

Once empty beaches were now often thronged with anglers, and the ready supply of bait was very much a thing of the past, with beaches crowded with anglers looking for bait that often they did not know how to dig! There were even professional bait diggers at Fraisthorpe who took everything that wriggled in their assault upon the rapidly diminishing bait beds. Such a loss of bait source can in any circumstances make going fishing even more difficult, and whereas once you could go into the Old Town of Filey and call upon a fishing family and buy whatever spare mussels they may have had, the loss of Filey's fishing fleet had sadly put an end to that. So, one had to find a retail source for bait and compete with a great many other anglers on the same search. This had its own difficulties, especially if you were, as I was, all over the county and rarely there to go and get the bait when it was available. Such is the problem of bait today that many sea anglers have aquariums that hold crabs (collected during the summer months), and these provide an excellent bait source when bait is particularly scarce. I once came up with an idea for an artificial lugworm that even today I am sure would work, but I could not get anyone interested on a professional basis.

And there was one other equally important problem: the disappearing beaches. In my lifetime Filey's wondrous beach has

211

dropped a good 3 feet in level and the quality of the beach is but a shadow of its former self. In my childhood, youth and as a young man when the beach had been reduced by easterly seas to rubble and small boulders that lay here there and everywhere, all over the beach, a full-blooded northerly sea would bring back the missing sand so that the beach looked as if it had been ironed level by an almighty hand, clean, level and back to its old appearance. Now most of Filey's sand lies in 'lays' (ridges of sand higher than the sand that surrounds them) in the bay itself or, much worse for Filey's beach, its lost sand lies on Smethwick Bank (which lies off Flamborough Head at the northern extremity of Bridlington Bay), waiting to be swept into Bridlington Bay to replenish its own missing sand beaches.

But just as bad for us was the disappearance of the beaches at Hilston. By 1975 the wonderful, wide and steep beach at the Hilston Road end had gone, washed away so that only a chequer-board pattern of boulder clay remained. You could fish from the cliff top at high water, but that was just not the same. What hurt just as much was that our much fished stretch of beach that lay beyond Hilston Road end, the even more wondrous beach at Turbot Hole and Rectory Steps (the Tunstall beach), had also been swept away.

We called this stretch of beach Little Dunge after the magnificent shingle beaches of the Dungeness peninsula. The Tunstall Dunge was about 400 yards long overall and so wide and steep that on a big tide if you were fortunate to have got a spot on Little Dunge you were standing sometimes as much as 40 yards from the cliff foot as the high water tide attacked the cliffs both north and south of you. This beach offered much to the thinking angler and many good fish were caught from it. Then, it too was washed away and the only places to fish were at Sand-le-Mere, the small boat landing and dock a mile south-east of Tunstall itself. None of this helped, and did little to tempt me even if I had had the time and opportunity to go fishing.

This seemed to be a most disappointing end to what had been an amazing and fulfilling fishing experience, but of course it was not an end. In the event I took up freshwater fishing – but that is another story altogether. Nor do I want to pontificate about fishing, sea fishing in particular, but the temptation is very great. Within my lifetime I have seen the almost total destruction of a natural wealth of creation, the sea and all that lives in it. Had I or any of my generation of sea anglers been told that this would happen when we began our journeys of sea fishing, I doubt few would have believed it. The wealth of sea fishing available today is but a fraction of what was available at the beginning of our lives. Greed and stupidity are the causes, of course.

Be in no doubt whatever, if we had treated the fair and pleasant land of the British Isles as we have treated the sea, there would be a sandy desert from John O'Groats to Land's End. The once mighty Herring fishery that at one time employed as many as 100,000 people is today hardly a smudge on the landscape. The destruction of the Sand Eels, one of the very keystones to the survival of both fish stocks and the seabirds, has gone virtually unnoticed, and other causes of the decline of fishstocks and bird deaths have been earnestly ignored by all the powers that be.

As a boy and young man I used to go to the cliff top, beginning in late May and through June and even July, to look for the signs of feeding seabids across Filey Bay. Those blizzards of white would be scattered in patches from beyond the Brig, down Tideway across the Bay as far as Flamborough Head end like daisies in a wide green field. That was the sign of the arrival and presence of both Sand Eels and Herring sile, a guarantee of the best of summer fishing for both man and birds. I have not seen a sight like that for at least 25 years if not more, a sure sign of the devastation caused by modern commercial fishing.

Maybe there is some truth in the effects of climate change on Sand Eels but there is a great deal more truth in the evidence of the effects of industrial fishing of Sand Eels where over 2 million tonnes of Sand Eels were taken without thought or care from the early nineties up to 2009 when finally some form of regulation was applied. You must remember that where Sand Eels are in evidence, and for that matter Herring, so also are most of the rest of the fish of the sea. One wonders just how many tonnes of white fish (Cod, Haddock, Coalfish and the rest) were taken with the Sand Eels!

I once held a baby Herring in the palm of my hand and, as I looked at it, I saw that the hollow of my hand was all but covered by a film of fine clear oil, so rich in oil is the Herring. Its nutritional values are legendary.

Incidentally, those industrial fishing nets would not have brought up just Sand Eels, but there would have been many tons of white fish as well … and when you think about the Mackerel fishing industry, words fail me. On holiday in the late 1980s, my wife and I visited Ullapool on a tour of north west Scotland. At anchor in Loch Broom were 37 East European, Polish, Soviet, East German and the rest, deep water trawlers with attendant mother ships. On enquiring I was told that the fleet were there for the 'Mackerel Klondyke'. Heaven alone knows just how many tonnes of Mackerel – and the rest! – were harvested by that lot. The town of Ullapool was full of crews of those ships, and not a policeman nor customs officer in sight! I was so appalled I wrote to my MP to complain.

My MP asked the appropriate government department for a response. The relevant government minister told him that having '… all the Klondykers spending their money in Ullapool was a deal better than the taxpayers having to pay out benefits to an area which would otherwise be in economic difficulty!' And that was just one area of the waters around the British Isles that has been plundered, not only by the Eastern Europeans but also by the Dutch, French, Spanish and the rest of the European fishing economies. No wonder the wondrous Mackerel fishing, by float or lure, of my youth is but a memory. A joyous one, but now long gone, maybe forever. You have been warned!

Acknowledgements

There are a number of people who I must thank for their help in writing this memoir. Some are no longer with us, in particular Bernard Venables and Clive Gammon, whose writings never failed to trigger my enthusiasm and entertained whilst they did it.

I extend my thanks to Mike Thrussell, Snr, of World Sea Fishing Forum who gave me the link to find Brian Harris, the retired editor of *Angling* magazine, and through Brian find a copy of 'Conger Rock', which is included in this book.

Most of the stories were written some time ago and had to be retyped so as to fit into this memoir. For this task I was blessed with the services of Hazel Allison, whose patience and ability to produce a useable printed story really did much to bring this book into reality.

And finally I must give thanks to and acknowledge the kindness shown by both *Angling* and *Dalesman* magazines in allowing me to use the stories that were originally included in their pages but are now included here.

To you all I express my profound thanks.